A-Z Street Atlas of BOURNEMOUTH

Key to Maps

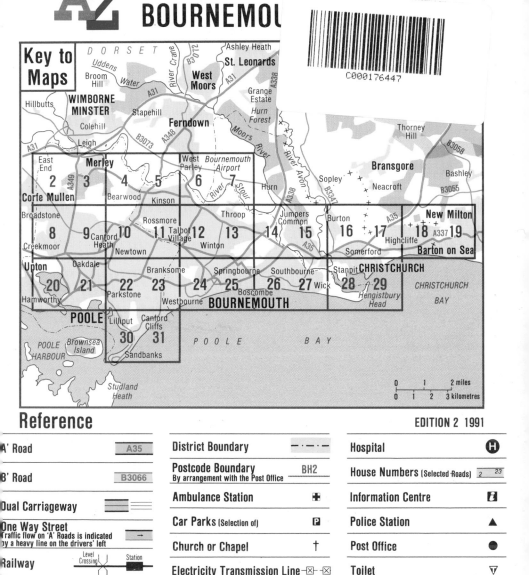

EDITION 2 1991

Reference

'A' Road	A35	
'B' Road	B3066	
Dual Carriageway		
One Way Street Traffic flow on 'A' Roads is indicated by a heavy line on the drivers' left	→	
Railway	Level Crossing / Station	
County Boundary	+ + +	
District Boundary	— · — · —	
Postcode Boundary By arrangement with the Post Office	BH2	
Ambulance Station	✚	
Car Parks (Selection of)	P	
Church or Chapel	†	
Electricity Transmission Line	—⊠—⊠	
Fire Station	■	
Hospital	H	
House Numbers (Selected Roads)	2 23	
Information Centre	i	
Police Station	▲	
Post Office	●	
Toilet	▽	
Disabled Toilet (National Key Scheme)	♿	

SCALE 4 inches to 1 mile

0 ¼ ½ mile
0 250 500 750 metres

1:15,840

© 1991 Copyright of the Publishers
Geographers' A-Z Map Company Limited

Head Office: Fairfield Road, Borough Green, Sevenoaks, Kent. TN15 8PP Telephone 0732 781000
Showrooms: 44 Gray's Inn Road, Holborn, London, WC1X 8LR. Telephone 071 242 9246
**The Maps in this atlas are based upon the Ordnance Survey Maps with the sanction of The Controller of Her Majesty's Stationery Office.
Crown Copyright Reserved.**

ISBN 0 85039 207 1

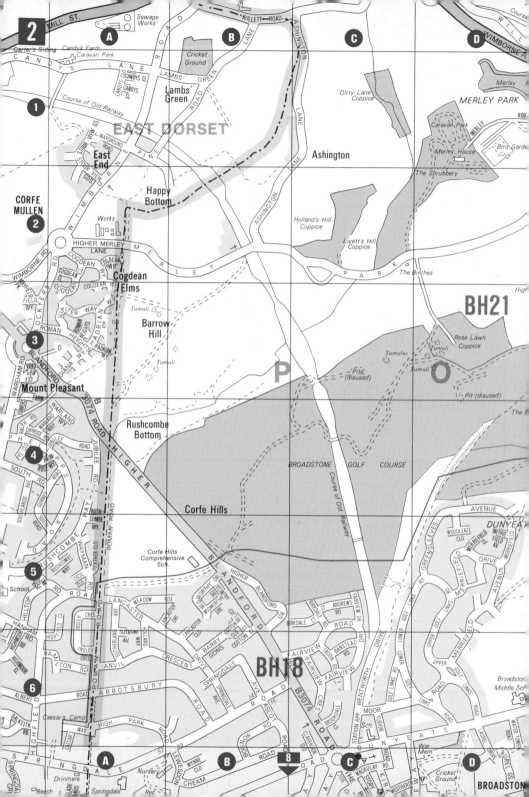

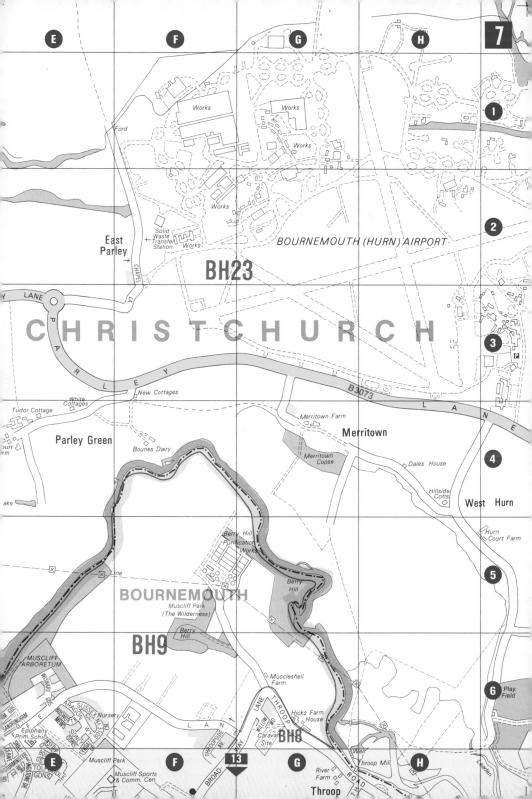

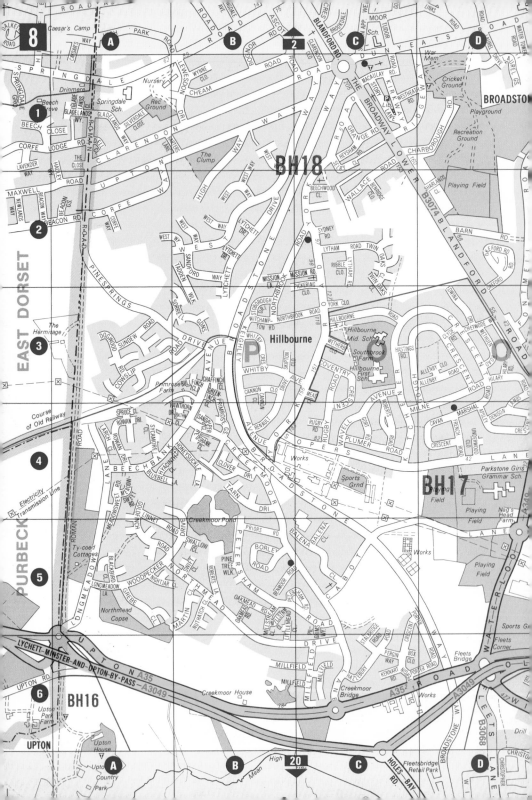

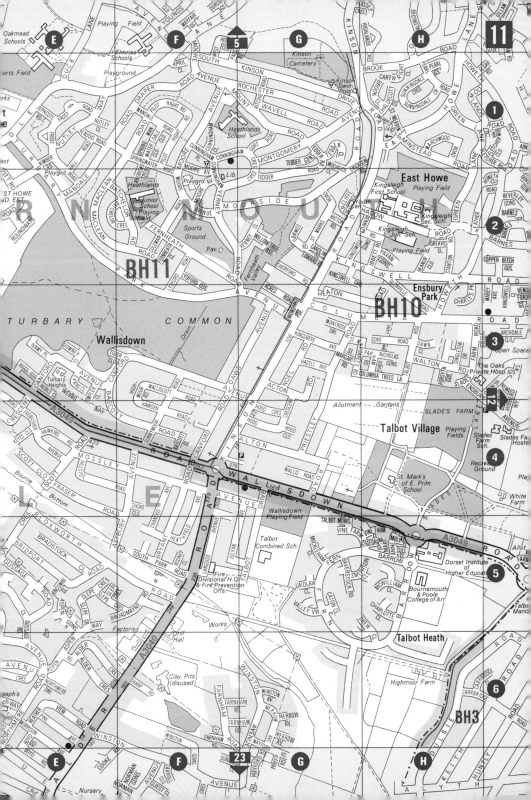

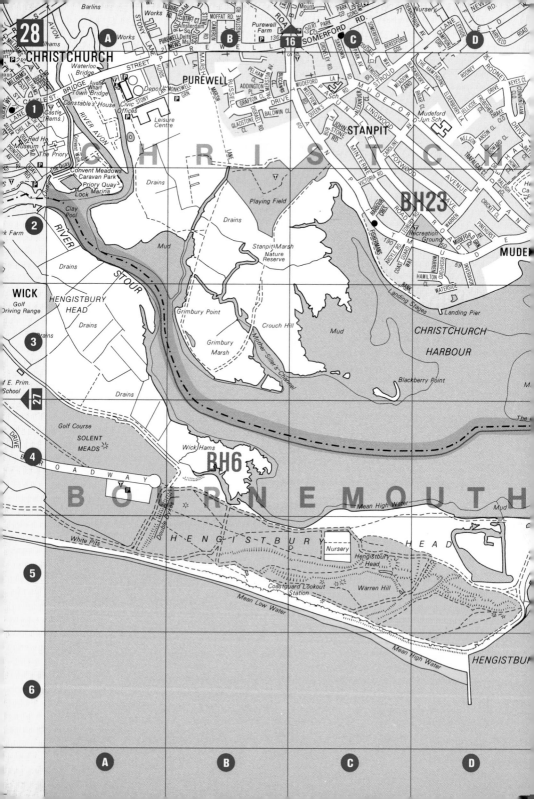

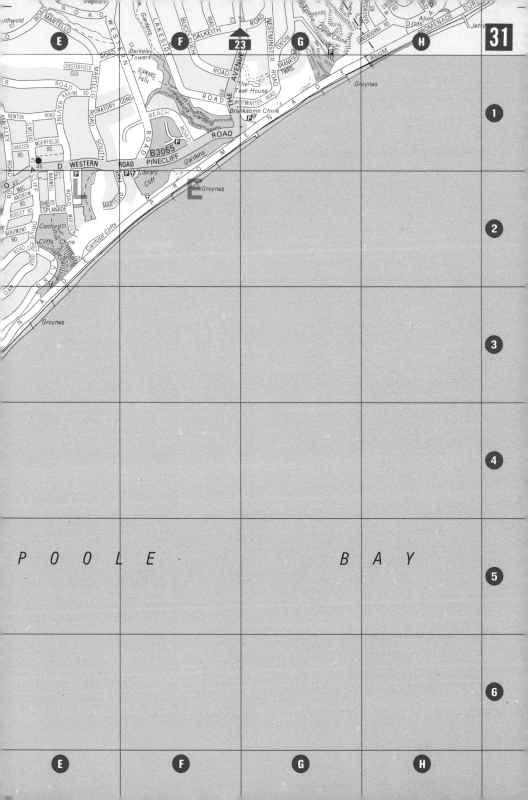

INDEX TO STREETS

HOW TO USE THIS INDEX

(a) A strict alphabetical order is followed in which Av., Rd., St., etc. are read in full and as part of the name preceding them; e.g. Avoncliffe Rd. follows Avon Bldgs. but precedes Avon Clo.

(b) Each street is followed by its Postal Code District Number and map reference; e.g. Aaron Clo. BH17—5G9 is in the Bournemouth 17 Postal Code District and is to be found in square 5G on page 9.

N.B. The Postal Code District Numbers given in this index are, in fact, only the first part of the Postcode to each address and are only meant to indicate the Postal Code District in which each street is situated.

ABBREVIATIONS USED IN THIS INDEX

All : Alley	Bldgs : Buildings	E : East	Ind : Industrial	N : North	Sq : Square
App : Approach	Chyd : Churchyard	Embkmt : Embankment	Junct : Junction	Pal : Palace	Sta : Station
Arc : Arcade	Cir : Circus	Est : Estate	La : Lane	Pde : Parade	St : Street
Av : Avenue	Clo : Close	Gdns : Gardens	Lit : Little	Pk : Park	Ter : Terrace
Bk : Back	Comn : Common	Ga : Gate	Lwr : Lower	Pas : Passage	Up : Upper
Boulevd : Boulevard	Cotts : Cottages	Gt : Great	Mans : Mansions	Pl : Place	Vs : Villas
BH : Bournemouth	Ct : Court	Grn : Green	Mkt : Market	Prom : Promenade	Wlk : Walk
Bri : Bridge	Cres : Crescent	Gro : Grove	M : Mews	Rd : Road	W : West
B'way : Broadway	Dri : Drive	Ho : House	Mt : Mount	S : South	Yd : Yard

Aaron Clo. BH17—5G 9
Abbotsbury Rd. BH18—6A 2
Abbots Clo. BH23—5A 18
Abbott Rd. BH9—5D 12
Abbott Rd. BH9—5D 12
Aberdare Rd. BH10—1B 12
Abingdon Dri. BH23—5D 18
Abingdon Rd. BH17—4F 9
Abinger Rd. BH7—1B 26
Abney Rd. BH10—1A 12
Acland Rd. BH9—5D 12
Acres Rd. BH11—3G 11
Acton Rd. BH10—3G 11
Adastral Rd. BH1—3G to 6F 9
Addington Pl. BH23—1B 28
Addiscombe Rd. BH23—2G 15
Adelaide Rd. BH15—4E 21
Adeline Rd. BH5—3G 25
Admirals Wlk. BH2—5A 24
Admiralty Rd. BH6—4F 27
(in two parts)
Airfield Rd. BH23—6D 16
Airfield Way. BH23—6D 16
Airspeed Rd. BH23—6F 17
Albany Clo. BH9—5C 12
Albemarle Rd. BH3—6C 12
Albert Rd. BH1—4C 24
Albert Rd. BH12—2C 22
Albert Rd. BH21—6A 2
Albert Rd. BH25—2G 19
Albion Clo. BH14—6A 10
Albion Rd. BH23—4F 15
Alby Rd. BH12—2E 23
Alcester Rd. BH12—1C 22
Alder Clo. BH24—4B 6
Alder Cres. BH12—6E 11
Alderley Rd. BH10—6A 6
Alderney Av. BH12—4C 10
Alder Rd. BH12—2D 22 to 4F 11
Aldis Gdns. BH15—4A 20
Aldridge Rd. BH10—6H 5
Alexander Clo. BH23—1C 28
Alexandra Rd. BH6—2C 26
Alexandra Rd. BH14—2C 22
Alford Rd. BH3—6A 12
Alington Clo. BH14—2C 30
Alington Rd. BH14—2B 30
Alipore Clo. BH14—4C 22
Allenby Clo. BH17—3D 8
Allenby Rd. BH17—3D 8
Alma Rd. BH9—6C 12
Almer Rd. BH15—4A 20
Almond Gro. BH12—5C 10
Alton Rd. BH10—4G 11
Alton Rd. BH14—4C 22
Alton Rd. E. BH14—5C 22
Alum Chine Rd. BH4—4G 23
Alumdale Rd. BH4—4G 23
Alumhurst Rd. BH4—4G 23
Alum Prom. BH4—6H 23
Alverston Av. BH15—4G 21

Alyth Rd. BH3—1H 23
Ambassador Clo. BH23—1E 29
Amberley Clo. BH23—4A 18
Amberwood. BH25—6E 19
Amberwood Clo. BH23—3B 18
Amberwood Dri. BH23—3B 18
Amberwood Gdns. BH23—3B 18
Ambleside. BH23—2E 15
Ambury La. BH23—5C 16
Amesbury Rd. BH6—1D 26
Amethyst Rd. BH23—5C 16
Ampfield Rd. BH8—1F 13
Amsterdam Sq. BH23—6B 16
Anchor Clo. BH11—5E 5
Anchor Clo. BH23—2E 29
Anchor Rd. BH11—6E 5
Andover Clo. BH23—6F 17
Andrews Clo. BH11—2F 11
Angeline Clo. BH23—5B 18
Anne Clo. BH23—4G 15
Annerley Rd. BH1—3E 25
Annet Clo. BH15—5A 20
Anson Clo. BH23—1D 28
Anstey Clo. BH11—5F 5
Anstey Rd. BH11—6F 5
Anthony's Av. BH14—1B 30
Anvil Clo. BH18—6A 2
Apollo Clo. BH12—6C 10
Apple Gro. BH23—3E 15
Appletree Clo. BH6—2C 26
Appletree Clo. BH25—4H 19
Approach Rd. BH14—4A 22
April Clo. BH11—1F 11
Apsley Cres. BH17—4D 8
Aragon Way. BH9—6E 7
Arcade, The. BH1—4C 24
Arcadia Av. BH8—5E 13
Arcadia Rd. BH23—4A 18
Archdale Clo. BH10—3A 12
Archway Rd. BH14—3D 22
Arden Rd. BH9—2C 12
Ardmore Rd. BH14—3A 22
Argyle Rd. BH23—2C 28
Argyll Rd. BH5—3G 25
Argyll Rd. BH12—1C 22
Ariel Clo. BH6—2H 27
Ariel Dri. BH6—2H 27
Arley Rd. BH14—5H 21
Arlington Rd. BH3—1D 24
Arne Av. BH12—6D 10
Arne Cres. BH12—6E 11
Arnewood Rd. BH6—2C 26
Arnolds Clo. BH25—5G 19
Arran Way. BH23—4D 18
Arrowsmith La. BH21—3F 3
Arrowsmith Rd. BH21—
—5E to 2H 3
Arthur Clo. BH2—2C 24
Arthur La. BH23—6G 15
Arthur Rd. BH23—6G 15

Arundel Clo. BH25—2F 19
Arundel Way. BH23—6A 18
Ascham Rd. BH6—2E 25
Ascot Rd. BH18—6B 2
Ashbourne Rd. BH5—2B 26
Ashdown Clo. BH17—4G 9
Ashford Rd. BH6—6D 14
Ashington La. BH21—1C 2
Ashley Clo. BH1—1G 25
Ashley Rd. BH1—1G 25
Ashley Rd. BH14—2A to 2D 22
Ashley Rd. BH25—2H 19
Ashling Clo. BH8—5E 13
Ashling Cres. BH8—4E 13
Ashmore Av. BH15—6B 20
Ashmore Av. BH25—5H 9
Ashmore Cres. BH15—6B 20
Ashmore Gro. BH23—4A 18
Ashridge Av. BH10—6A 6
Ashridge Gdns. BH10—6A 6
Ashridge Pde. BH10—5A 6
Ashton Rd. BH9—2B 12
Ashurst Rd. BH8—1F 13
Ashwood Dri. BH18—6E 3
Aspen Gdns. BH12—5E 11
Aspen Pl. BH25—4H 19
Aspen Rd. BH12—6E 11
Aspen Way. BH12—6E 11
Astbury Av. BH17—5A 8
Aston Mead. BH23—1E 15
Athelstan Rd. BH6—2E 27
Auckland Rd. BH23—6G 17
Austen Av. BH10—5A 6
Auster Clo. BH23—6E 17
Austin Av. BH14—6A 22
Austin Clo. BH1—2G 25
Avalon. BH14—1B 30
Avebury Av. BH10—5A 6
Avenue La. BH2—4B 24
Avenue Rd. BH2—4B 24
Avenue Rd. BH23—6F 15
(Christchurch)
Avenue Rd. BH23—3D 18
(Walkford)
Avenue Rd. BH25—2H 19
Avenue, The. BH9—2C 12
Avenue, The. BH13
—1F 31 to 4G 23
Avon Bldgs. BH23—6H 15
Avoncliffe Rd. BH6—4E 27
Avon Clo. BH8—1F 25
Avon Rd. BH8—1F 25
Avon Rd. E. BH23—5G 15
Avon Rd. W. BH23—5F 15
Avon Run Clo. BH23—2F 29
Avon Run Rd. BH23—2F 29
Avon View Pde. BH23—2A 16
Avon View Rd. BH23—2A 16
Avon Wharf. BH23—1A 28
Axford Clo. BH8—2G 13

Aylesbury Rd. BH1—3G 25

Bath Rd. BH1—5C 24
Baverstock Rd. BH12—5G 11
Bay Hog La. BH15—5D 20
Baytree Way. BH23—3H 17
Bay View. BH25—6D 18
Beach Av. BH25—6G 19
Beach Rd. BH13—1F 31
Balcombe Rd. BH13—3F 23
Baldwin Clo. BH23—1B 28
Balena Clo. BH17—5C 8
Balfour Clo. BH23—4G 17
Balfour Rd. BH9—3C 12
Ballard Clo. BH15—6E 21
Ballard Clo. BH25—1H 19
Ballard Rd. BH15—6E 21
Balmoral Av. BH8—4H 13
Balmoral Rd. BH14—4B 22
Balmoral Wlk. BH25—2G 19
Balston Rd. BH14—1A 22
Bank Clo. BH23—1H 27
Bankside Rd. BH9—2B 12
Banks Rd. BH13—6A to 4D 30
Banstead Rd. BH18—6C 2
Bargates. BH23—6G 15
Baring Rd. BH6—3G 27
Barlands Clo. BH23—2A 16
Barnes Clo. BH10—2A 12
Barnes Cres. BH10—2A 12
Barnes Rd. BH10—2A 12
Barnfield. BH23—5G 17
Barn Rd. BH18—2D 8
Barons Rd. BH11—5C 4
Barrack Rd. BH23
—5D 14 to 1H 27
Barrie Rd. BH9—2C 12
Barrington Ct. BH3—5A 12
Barrow Dri. BH8—3H 13
Barrowgate Rd. BH8—2F 13
Barrowgate Way. BH8—1F 13
Barrow Rd. BH8—3H 13
Barrow Way. BH8—3H 13
Bars Av. BH25—1H 19
Barry Gdns. BH18—6B 2
Barters La. BH18—1A 8
Bartlett Dri. BH7—5C 14
Barton Ct. Av. BH25—6D 19
Barton Ct. Rd. BH25—4H 19
Barton Croft. BH25—6F 19
Barton Dri. BH25—5G 19
Barton La. BH25—4F 19
Bartonside Rd. BH25—5D 18
Barton Way. BH25—5G 19
Barton Wood Rd. BH25—6F 19
Bascott Clo. BH11—4F 11
Bascott Rd. BH11—3E 11
Bashley Cross Rd. BH23—1C 18
Bassett Rd. BH12—1B 22
Batchelor Cres. BH11—2F 11
Batchelor Rd. BH11—2F 11
Batcombe Clo. BH11—1D 10
Bath Hill Ct. BH1—4C 24

Belvedere Rd. BH23—6G 15
Bemister Rd. BH9—5C 12
Benbow Cres. BH12—3D 10
Benbridge Av. BH11—6E 5
Bendigo Rd. BH23—4E 15
Benellen Av. BH4—3A 23
Benellen Gdns. BH4—3H 23
Benellen Rd. BH4—2H 23
Benellen Towers. BH4—3H 23
Bengal Rd. BH9—4B 12
Benmore Rd. BH17—5B 8
Benmore Rd. BH9—4C 12
Bennett Rd. BH8—1E 25
Bennion Rd. BH10—2H 11
Benridge Clo. BH17—5G 9
Bentley Rd. BH9—2C 12
Bere Clo. BH17—2F 9
Beresford Clo. BH12—1C 22
Beresford Gdns. BH23—6C 16
Beresford Rd. BH6—3C 26
Beresford Rd. BH12—1C 22
Berkeley Av. BH12—5C 10
Berkeley Rd. BH3—6B 12
Bernards Clo. BH23—5E 15
Berrans Av. BH11—5E 5
Berwick Rd. BH3—1B 24
Bessborough Rd. BH13—2D 30
Beswick Av. BH10—3A 12
Bethia Clo. BH8—6G 13
Bethia Rd. BH8—6G 13
Bettiscombe Clo. BH17—3F 9
Beverley Gdns. BH10—2A 12
Bexington Clo. BH11—1D 10
Bicton Rd. BH11—2G 11
Bindon Clo. BH12—6D 10
Bingham Av. BH14—2C 30
Bingham Clo. BH23—6C 16
Bingham Rd. BH9—5C 12
Bingham Rd. BH23—6C 16
Binnie Rd. BH12—2D 22
Birch Av. BH22—1B 6
Birch Av. BH23—2A 16
Birch Clo. BH14—4C 22
Birch Dri. BH8—3B 14
Birchwood Clo. BH23—4A 18
Birchwood Dri. BH14—2C 30
Birchwood M. BH14—4C 22
Birchwood Rd. BH14—4C 22
Birds Hill Rd. BH15—3F 21
Birkdale Ct. BH18—5C 2
Birkdale Rd. BH18—5C 2
Bishop Rd. BH9—5D 12
Bishops Clo. BH7—6G 13
—3C 26 to 2F 27
Blackberry La. BH23—1C 28
Blackbird Clo. BH17—5A 8
Blackburn Rd. BH12—1A 22
Blackfield Rd. BH8—1G 13
Blackwater Dri. BH23—3E 3
Blair Av. BH14—3B 22
Blair Clo. BH25—1G 19
Blake Dene Rd. BH14—6B 22

Blake Hill Av. BH14—6C 22
Blake Hill Cres. BH14—6B 22
Blandford Rd. BH15
　—3A to 6C 20
Blandford Rd. BH21—3A 2
Blenheim Dri. BH23—6E 17
Bloomfield Av. BH9—2C 12
Bloxworth Rd. BH12—5E 11
Bluebell Clo. BH23—5F 17
Bluebell La. BH17—4A 8
Blyth Clo. BH27—1D 14
Blythswood Ct. BH25—6H 19
Bodley Rd. BH13—2E 30
Bodorgan Rd. BH2—3C 24
Bodowen Clo. BH23—3B 16
Bodowen Rd. BH23—3B 16
Bognor Rd. BH18—1B 8
Boldre Clo. BH12—6D 10
Boleyn Cres. BH9—6E 7
Bolton Clo. BH6—4E 27
Bolton Rd. BH6—4E 27
Bond Rd. BH15—2G 21
Bonham Rd. BH9—6C 12
Bonington Clo. BH23—5C 16
Boreham Rd. BH6—1D 26
Borley Rd. BH17—5B 8
Borthwick Rd. BH1—2G 25
Boscombe Cliff Rd. BH5—4H 25
Boscombe Gro. Rd. BH1—2G 25
Boscombe Overcliff Dri. BH5
　—4A 26
Boscombe Prom. BH5—4G 25
Boscombe Spa Rd. BH5—3G 25
Bosley Clo. BH20—3E 15
Bosley Way. BH23—3E 15
Bosworth M. BH6—2F 12
Boulnois Av. BH14—4D 22
Boundary Rd. BH12—5A 12
Bourne Av. BH2—3B 24
Bourne Clo. BH2—4A 24
Bournemouth Rd. BH14
　—3A 22 to 2E 23
Bourne Valley Rd. BH12—2F 23
Bournewood Dri. BH4—3H 23
Bourton Gdns. BH7—5E 14
Bouverie Clo. BH25—4H 19
Boveridge Gdns. BH9—1E 13
Bovington Clo. BH17—3H 9
Bowden Rd. BH12—3B 10
Bower Rd. BH8—5G 13
Box Clo. BH17—6C 8
Boyd Rd. BH12—1A 22
Brabazon Rd. BH21—1H 3
Brabazon Rd. BH23—6F 17
Brackendale Rd. BH8—5F 13
Bracken Glen. BH15—2F 21
Brackenhill. BH13—2F 23
Bracken Rd. BH6—3C 26
Bracken Way. BH23—4C 18
Bradburne Rd. BH2—4B 24
Bradbury Clo. BH18—1E 9
Bradford Rd. BH9—1F 13
Bradpole Rd. BH8—3G 13
Bradstock Clo. BH17—5E 11
Braemar Av. BH6—3G 27
Braemar Clo. BH6—3G 27
Braemar Dri. BH23—4A 18
Braidley Rd. BH2—3B 24
Brailswood Rd. BH15—3F 21
Braishfield Gdns. BH8—3G 13
Bramble La. BH23—4C 18
Bramley Rd. BH10—5H 5
Brampton Rd. BH15—1F 21
Bramshaw. BH25—6E 19
Bramshaw Rd. BH8—2G 13
Branders Clo. BH6—3G 27
Branders La. BH6—2G 27
Branksea Av. BH15—6A 20
Branksea Clo. BH15—6A 20
Branksome Dene Rd. BH4
　—5G 23
Branksome Hill Rd. BH4—2G 23
Branksome Towers. BH13
　—1G 31

Branksome Wood Gdns. BH2
　—3A 24
Branksome Wood Rd. BH4, BH2 &
　BH12—2G 23
Branwell Clo. BH23—4G 15
Brassey Clo. BH9—4D 12
Brassey Rd. BH9—3C 12
Breamore Clo. BH15—2G 19
Brecon Clo. BH10—5B 6
Bredy Clo. BH17—4F 9
Bremble Clo. BH12—3C 10
Brendon Rd. BH8—3G 13
Briar Clo. BH15—2F 21
Briar Clo. BH23—1D 28
Brickenswood. BH25—5E 19
Bridge App. BH15—6C 20
Bridge Pl. BH10—4A 6
Bridge Rd. BH23—1A 28
Bridgewater Rd. BH12—1C 22
Bridle Cres. BH7—5D 14
Bridport Rd. BH12—5E 11
Brierley Av. BH22—1B 6
Brierley Clo. BH10—6B 6
Brierley Rd. BH10—1A 12
Brightlands Av. BH6—2F 27
Bright Rd. BH15—1F 21
Brinsons Clo. BH23—2A 16
Brisbane Rd. BH23—4E 15
Britannia Rd. BH14—4H 21
Britannia Way. BH23—6E 17
Brixey Clo. BH12—5B 10
Brixey Rd. BH12—6B 10
Broad Av. BH8—4G 13
Broadhurst Av. BH10—1B 12
Broadlands Av. BH6—3G 27
Broadlands Clo. BH8—2G 13
Broadlands Clo. BH23—3D 18
Broadmayne Rd. BH12—5E 11
Broadstone Way. BH18
　—2B 8 to 1D 20
Broadwater Av. BH14—5B 22
Broadway La. BH8—2E 13
Broadway, The. BH10—5A 6
Broadway, The. BH18—1C 8
Brockenhurst Rd. BH23—4F 15
Brockley Rd. BH10—1A 12
Bronte Av. BH23—4G 15
Brook Av. BH25—1H 19
Brookdale Clo. BH18—6C 2
Brooke Clo. BH10—1H 11
Brooklyn Ct. BH25—2H 19
Brook Rd. BH10—1H 11
Brook Rd. BH12—2B 22
Brookside Way. BH23—3A 18
Brook Way. BH23—6F 17
Broom Rd. BH12—4B 10
Broughton Av. BH10—1B 12
Broughton Clo. BH10—1B 12
Brownen Rd. BH9—5D 12
Browning Av. BH5—2A 26
Browning Rd. BH12—1C 22
Brownsea Clo. BH25—2G 19
Brownsea Rd. BH13—1D 30
Brownsea View Av. BH14
　—6B 22
Brudenell Av. BH13—2C 30
Brudenell Rd. BH13—2C 30
Brunstead Pl. BH12—3F 23
Brunstead Rd. BH12—3F 23
Bryanstone Rd. BH3—5B 12
Bryant Rd. BH12—5F 11
Bub La. BH23—1C 28
Buccaneers Clo. BH23—1B 28
Buccleuch Rd. BH13—6F 23
Buce Hayes Clo. BH23—5B 18
Buchanan Av. BH7—1G 25
Buckingham Rd. BH12—6D 10
Buckingham Wlk. BH25—2G 19
Buckland Gro. BH23—2H 17
Buckland Rd. BH12—2B 22
Buckland Ter. BH12—2C 22
Bucklers Way. BH8—2F 13
Buckthorn Clo. BH17—4B 8

Bullfinch Clo. BH17—3B 8
Burbridge Clo. BH17—5C 9
Burcombe Rd. BH10—6H 5
Bure Clo. BH23—1F 29
Bure Haven Dri. BH23—1E 29
Bure Homage Gdns. BH23
　—1E 29
Bure Homage La. BH23—1E 29
Bure La. BH23—2E 29
Bure Pk. BH23—6F 17
Bure Rd. BH23—1F 29
Burford Clo. BH23—4D 14
Burleigh Rd. BH6—1D 26
Burley Rd. BH12—1B 22
Burlington Arc., The. BH1
　—4C 24
Burnaby Rd. BH4—6H 23
Burnbrae Rd. BH22—1A 22
Burnett Av. BH23—5E 15
Burnett Rd. BH23—5E 15
Burngate Rd. BH15—5A 20
Burnham Dri. BH8—5F 13
Burnham Rd. BH23—2A 16
Burnside. BH23—5H 17
Burns Rd. BH6—6E 15
Burtley Rd. BH6—4F 27
Burton Clo. BH23—1A 16
Burtoncroft. BH23—1A 16
Burton Hall Pl. BH23—2A 16
Burton Rd. BH13—4F 23
Burton Rd. BH23—6C 16
Bury Rd. BH13—5E 23
Bushell Rd. BH15—6D 8
Bushey Rd. BH8—4E 13
Bute Dri. BH23—5D 18
Buttercup Dri. BH23—4F 17
Byron Rd. BH25—3H 25

Cabot La. BH17—5C 8
Cabot Way. BH25—1G 19
Cadhay Clo. BH25—2G 19
Cadnam Way. BH8—2G 13
Caesar's Way. BH18—6A 2
Cairns Clo. BH23—4F 15
Calder Rd. BH17—4G 9
Caledonian Clo. BH23—6F 17
Caledon Rd. BH14—4D 22
Calmore Clo. BH8—2F 13
Calvin Rd. BH9—4C 12
Cambridge Gdns. BH23—3F 15
Cambridge Rd. BH2—4A 24
Camden Clo. BH9—3D 12
Camellia Gdns. BH25—2H 19
Cameron Rd. BH23—6B 16
Cammel Rd. BH22—1A 6
Campbell Rd. BH1—2G 25
Campbell Rd. BH23—2A 16
Campion Gro. BH23—6D 16
Canberra Rd. BH23—4E 15
Candys Clo. BH21—1A 2
Candy's La. BH21—1A 2
Canford Av. BH11—3E 11
Canford Cliffs Av. BH14—5D 22
Canford Cliffs Rd. BH13—1D 30
Canford Cres. BH13—3D 30
Canford Heath Rd. BH17
　—3E 9 to 2A 10
Canford Magna. BH21—1H 3
Canford Rd. BH11—4F 11
Canford Rd. BH15—3E 21
Canford Way. BH12—3B 10
Cannon Clo. BH18—3B 8
Capesthorne. BH23—2F 29
Capstone Pl. BH8—1F 25
Capstone Rd. BH8—6D 12
Carbery Av. BH6—3D 26
Carbery Gdns. BH6—2E 27
Carbery La. BH6—3D 26
Cardigan Rd. BH9—5C 12
Cardigan Rd. BH22—2E 23
Carey Rd. BH9—2C 12
Careys Rd. BH8—1F 13
Carisbrooke Ct. BH25—2G 19

Carisbrooke Cres. BH15—4A 20
Carisbrooke Way. BH23—4A 18
Carlton Av. BH25—5F 19
Carlton Gro. BH12—2C 22
Carlton Rd. BH1—3F 25
Carlyle Rd. BH6—6D 14
Carnarvon Rd. BH1—3G 25
Caroline Av. BH23—1C 28
Caroline Rd. BH11—2G 11
Carrbridge Clo. BH8—6H 11
Carrbridge Rd. BH3—6H 11
Carroll Clo. BH12—1F 23
Carsworth Way. BH17—3H 9
Carters Av. BH15—3A 20
Carters La. BH24—2A 22
Cartwright Clo. BH10—1H 11
Carysgort Rd. BH1—2G 25
Caslake Clo. BH25—4H 19
Cassel Av. BH13 & BH4—6G 23
Castle Av. BH23—5A 18
Castle Dene Cres. BH14—5H 21
Castle Ga. Clo. BH8—5F 13
Castle Hill. BH14—3A 22
Castle La. E. BH7—4B 14
Castle La. W. BH9 & BH8
　—1D 12 to 4A 14
Castlemain Av. BH6—2C 26
Castle Pde. BH7—5D 14
Castle Rd. BH9—4C 12
Castle St. BH15—6D 20
Castle St. BH23—1H 27
Castleton Av. BH10—4A 6
Catalina Clo. BH23—6D 16
Catalina Dri. BH15—6F 21
Caton Clo. BH12—5G 11
Cattistock Rd. BH8—3G 13
Cavan Cres. BH17—4D 8
Cavendish Pl. BH1—2C 24
Cavendish Rd. BH1—2C 24
Caversham Clo. BH15—4A 20
Cawdor Rd. BH3—6A 12
Caxton Clo. BH23—6D 16
Cecil Av. BH8—6E 13
Cecil Clo. BH21—5A 2
Cecil Hill. BH8—5E 13
Cecil Rd. BH5—3G 25
Cecil Rd. BH12—1D 22
Cedar Av. BH10—5A 6
Cedar Av. BH23—4D 14
Celandine Clo. BH23—5F 17
Cellars Farm Rd. BH6—4G 27
Cemetery Av. BH15—1D 22
Central Av. BH12—1D 22
Central Dri. BH2—3B 24
Cerne Clo. BH9—1E 13
Chaddesley Glen. BH13—3D 30
Chaddesley Wood Rd. BH13
　—4D 30
Chaffinch Clo. BH17—3B 8
Chalbury Clo. BH17—3A 10
Chaldecott Gdns. BH10—1H 11
Chaldon Rd. BH17—3H 9
Chalfont Av. BH23—1E 15
Chandlers Clo. BH7—5B 14
Chandos Av. BH12—5F 11
Channel Ct. BH25—6F 19
Chantry Clo. BH23—3A 18
Chapel La. BH15—5D 20
Chapel La. BH22—2F 7
Chapel Rd. BH14—3H 21
Charborough Rd. BH18—1C 8
Charles Pk. BH10—3H 11
Charles Rd. BH15—2F 21
Charles Rd. BH23—5D 16
Charlotte Clo. BH12—5H 11
Charlotte Clo. BH23—1E 29
Charlton Clo. BH9—1E 13
Charminster Av. BH9—4D 12
Charminster Clo. BH8—3E 13
Charminster Pl. BH8—3E 13
Charminster Rd. BH8
　—1C 24 to 2E 13
Charmouth Gro. BH14—3A 22
Charnwood Av. BH9—2D 12

Charter Rd. BH11—5D 4
Chaseside. BH7—5A 14
Chatsworth Rd. BH8—6E 13
Chatsworth Rd. BH14—2A 22
Chatsworth Way. BH25—1F 19
Chaucer Rd. BH13—1E 31
Cheam Rd. BH18—1B 8
Cheddington Rd. BH9—1D 12
Chedington Clo. BH17—3F 9
Cheltenham Rd. BH12—1B 22
Cherford Rd. BH11—2G 11
Cherita Ct. BH15—1G 21
Cheriton Av. BH7—5C 14
Cherries Dri. BH9—3B 12
Cherry Clo. BH14—2A 22
Cherry Tree Wlk. BH4—5A 24
Cheshire Dri. BH8—3B 14
Chesildene Av. BH8—2F 13
Chesildene Dri. BH8—2F 13
Cressel Av. BH5—2A 26
Chesterfield Clo. BH13—1E 31
Chester Rd. BH13—5F 23
Chestnut Av. BH6—3C 26
Chestnut Av. BH23—5D 14
Chestnut Av. BH25—5H 19
Chestnut Way. BH23—2A 16
Chetnole Clo. BH17—3H 9
Chetwode Way. BH17—3D 8
Chewton Comn. Rd. BH23
　—4B 18
Chewton Farm Rd. BH23—4B 18
Chewton Lodge. BH23—5D 18
Chewton Way. BH23—4C 18
Cheyne Gdns. BH4—5H 23
Chicherell Clo. BH9—1E 13
Chichester Wlk. BH21—1G 3
Chichester Way. BH23—2E 29
Chideock Clo. BH12—1D 22
Chigwell Rd. BH8—4E 13
Chilcombe Rd. BH6—1C 26
Chilfrome Clo. BH17—4E 9
Chiltern Clo. BH4—1G 23
Chiltern Dri. BH4—1G 23
Chiltern Dri. BH25—4F 19
Chine Cres. BH2—5A 24
Chine Cres. Rd. BH2—5A 24
Chine Wlk. BH22—1B 6
Chorley Clo. BH15—1E 21
Christchurch Bay Rd. BH25
　—6G 19
Christchurch By-Pass. BH23
　—6H 15 to 5E 17
Christchurch Rd. BH1 & BH7
　—4D 24 to 6D 14
Christchurch Rd. BH22
　—1G 5 & 3D 6
Christchurch Rd. BH25—5E 19
Christopher Cres. BH15—1D 20
Churchfield Cres. BH15—3G 21
Churchfield Rd. BH15—4F 21
Churchill Ct. BH25—2H 19
Churchill Cres. BH12—1C 22
Churchill Rd. BH1—2G 25
Churchill Rd. BH12—2C 22
Church La. BH22—4B 6
Church La. BH23—1H 27
Church La. BH25—4G 19
Church Rd. BH6—4F 27
Church Rd. BH14—3H 21
Church St. BH15—6D 20
Church St. BH23—1H 27
Cinnamon La. BH15—6D 20
Circle, The. BH9—1C 12
Circle, The. BH23—2E 31
Claremont Av. BH9—3E 13
Claremont Rd. BH9—3E 13
Clarence Pk. Rd. BH7—1G 25
Clarence Rd. BH14—4H 21
Clarendon Clo. BH18—6G 2
Clarendon Rd. BH4—5H 23
Clarendon Rd. BH18—1A 8
Clarendon Rd. BH23—3C 18
Clayford Clo. BH17—3E 9
Cleeves Clo. BH12—3C 10

Cleveland Clo. BH25—6F 19
Cleveland Gdns. BH1—2F 25
Cleveland Rd. BH1—2F 25
Cliff Dri. BH23—2E 31
Cliffe Dri. BH23—1G 29
Cliffe Rd. BH25—6F 19
Clifford Rd. BH9—3D 12
Cliff Ter. BH25—6G 19
Clifton Rd. BH6—4D 26
Clifton Rd. BH14—5C 22
Clingan Rd. BH6—6D 14
Clinton Clo. BH23—3C 18
Clive Rd. BH9—4C 12
Clive Rd. BH23—3H 17
Close, The. BH18—1A 8
Clover Clo. BH23—4F 17
Clover Dri. BH17—4B 8
Clowes Av. BH6—4H 27
Clyde Rd. BH17—3D 8
Coach Ho. Pl. BH8—2D 24
Coast Guard Way. BH23—2C 28
Cobbs La. BH15—1F 21
Cobham Rd. BH9—2D 12
Cobham Way. BH21—1F 3
Cockerell Clo. BH21—1G 3
Cogdean Clo. BH21—3A 2
Cogdean Rd. BH17—3F 9
Cogdean Way. BH21—2A 2
Colbourne Clo. BH15—6F 21
Colehill Cres. BH9—1E 13
Coleman Rd. BH11—2F 11
Colemere Gdns. BH23—4A 18
Colemore Rd. BH7—6C 14
Coleridge Grn. BH23—5D 16
Coles Av. BH15—5A 20
Coles Gdns. BH15—5A 20
College Rd. BH5—3B 26
Collingbourne Av. BH6—6D 14
Collwood Clo. BH15—6E 9
Colonnade Rd. BH5—2A 26
Columbia Rd. BH10—3G 11
Columbia Trees La. BH10
　—3H 11
Colville Rd. BH5—2A 26
Comber Rd. BH9—2C 12
Comet Way. BH23—6E 17
Comley Rd. BH9—3B 12
Commercial Rd. BH2—4B 24
Commercial Rd. BH14—3G 21
Compton Av. BH14—5C 22
Compton Dri. BH14—5C 22
Compton Gdns. BH14—5C 22
Compton Rd. BH25—3H 19
Conifer Av. BH14—5A 22
Conifer Clo. BH22—1B 6
Conifer Clo. BH23—2D 14
Coniston Av. BH11—5E 5
Connaught Clo. BH25—4F 19
Connaught Cres. BH12—1D 20
Connaught Rd. BH7—1B 26
Connell Rd. BH15—2D 20
Consort Clo. BH12—2B 22
Constitution Hill Rd. BH14
　—3G 21
Convent Meadows Caravan Pk.
　BH23—2A 28
Convent Wlk. BH23—1A 28
Conways Dri. BH14—3H 21
Cooke Rd. BH12—1E 23
Coombe Av. BH10—2B 12
Coombe Gdns. BH10—2A 12
Cooper Dean Dri. BH8—4A 14
Copeland Dri. BH14—5A 22
Copper Beech Gdns. BH10
　—2A 12
Coppice, The. BH23—1E 29
Coppice View. BH10—2B 12
Copse Clo. BH14—4H 21
Copse Way. BH23—2D 14
Copsewood Av. BH8—4H 13
Copythorne Clo. BH8—3G 13
Corbar Rd. BH23—5E 15
Corbiere Av. BH12—3C 10
Corfe Lodge Rd. BH18—1A 8

Corfe View La. BH14—4B 22
Corfe Way. BH18—2A 8
Corhampton Rd. BH6—1C 26
Cornelia Cres. BH12—1F 23
Cornford Way. BH23—5H 17
Cornish Gdns. BH10—3A 12
Coronation Av. BH9—3C 12
Corporation Rd. BH1—2E 25
Corscombe Clo. BH17—2F 9
Cotes Av. BH14—2H 21
Cotlands Rd. BH1—3E 25
Cotton Clo. BH18—5B 2
Countess Clo. BH21—2F 3
Countess Gdns. BH7—5A 14
Court Clo. BH23—6C 16
Courtenay Rd. BH14—3A 22
Courthill Rd. BH14—3C 22
Court Rd. BH9—4D 12
Covena Rd. BH6—1E 27
Coventry Cres. BH17—3C 8
Cove Rd. BH10—3H 11
Cowdrey Gdns. BH8—2A 14
Cowell Dri. BH7—5B 14
Cowley Rd. BH17—5F 9
Cowleys Rd. BH23—2A 16
Cowper Av. BH25—4H 19
Cowper Rd. BH9—3C 12
Cowslip Rd. BH18—3A 8
Cox Av. BH9—1D 12
Cox Clo. BH9—1D 12
Coy Pond Rd. BH12—2F 23
Crabton Clo. BH5—3A 26
Crabtree Clo. BH23—3A 16
Craigmoor Av. BH8—4H 13
Craigmoor Clo. BH8—4H 13
Craigmoor Way. BH8—3H 13
Cranborne Cres. BH12—5D 10
Cranborne Pl. BH25—1G 19
Cranborne Rd. BH2—5B 24
Cranbrook Rd. BH12—2A 22
Cranemoor Av. BH23—3A 18
Cranemoor Clo. BH23—3A 18
Cranemoor Gdns. BH23—3A 18
Crane's M. BH15—4E 21
Cranleigh Clo. BH6—2F 27
Cranleigh Gdns. BH6—2F 27
Cranleigh Rd. BH6—2D 26
Cranmer Rd. BH9—5C 12
Crantock Gro. BH8—3H 13
Cranwell Rd. BH11—1D 10
Crawshaw Rd. BH14—5A 22
Creasey Rd. BH11—5F 5
Creech Rd. BH12—2B 22
Creedy Path. BH23—1H 15
Creekmoor La. BH17—4B 8
Crescent Dri. BH25—6G 19
Crescent Rd. BH2—4B 24
Crescent Rd. BH14—3D 22
Crescent, The. BH1—3G 25
Crescent, The. BH25—5E 19
Crescent Wlk. BH22—1B 6
Cresta Gdns. BH22—1B 6
Crest Rd. BH12—1B 22
Cribb Clo. BH17—5G 9
Crichell Rd. BH9—5C 12
Crichel Mt. Rd. BH14—2B 30
Cricket Clo. BH23—2D 28
Crimea Rd. BH9—6C 12
Cringle Av. BH6—2C 27
Crispin Clo. BH23—5B 18
Crofton Clo. BH23—4F 15
Croft Rd. BH9—3B 12
Croft Rd. BH12—1A 22
Croft Rd. BH23—6D 16
Cromer Rd. BH8—6F 13
Cromer Rd. BH12—2E 23
Cromwell Pl. BH5—2B 26
Cromwell Rd. BH5—2B 26
Cromwell Rd. BH12—2C 22
Crosby Rd. BH4—6H 23
Crossmead Av. BH25—3H 19
Cross Way. BH23—4D 14
Crown Clo. BH12—2B 22
Crusader Ct. BH14—3G 23

Crusader Rd. BH11—6C 4
Cucklington Cres. BH9—1E 13
Cuckoo Rd. BH17—5H 9
Cudnell Av. BH11—5E 5
Cul-de-Sac. BH25—5E 19
Culford Clo. BH8—3H 13
Cull Clo. BH12—5H 11
Culliford Cres. BH17—3F 9
Culver Rd. BH25—3G 19
Cumnor Rd. BH1—3F 25
Cunningham Clo. BH11—1F 11
Cunningham Clo. BH23—1D 28
Cunningham Cres. BH11—1F 11
Cunningham Pl. BH11—1F 11
Curlew Rd. BH8—3F 13
Curlew Rd. BH23—1E 29
Curlieu Rd. BH15—1F 21
Curtis Rd. BH12—2B 22
Curzon Rd. BH1—1G 25
Curzon Rd. BH14—4A 22
Curzon Way. BH23—5H 17
Cynthia Clo. BH12—6A 10
Cynthia Rd. BH12—6A 10
Cyril Rd. BH8—1E 25

Dakota Clo. BH23—6F 17
Dale Clo. BH15—6G 9
Dale Rd. BH15—1H 21
Dale Valley Rd. BH15—6F 9
Dalewood Av. BH11—6D 4
Dalkeith La. BH1—4C 24
Dalkeith Rd. BH13—6F 23
Dalkeith Rd. BH2—6A 2
Dalling Rd. BH12—2F 23
Dalmeny Rd. BH6—4G 27
Damerham Rd. BH8—2G 13
Danecourt Clo. BH14—3G 21
Danecourt Rd. BH14—3G 21
Danesbury Av. BH6—3F 27
Danes Clo. BH25—6H 19
Dansie Clo. BH14—3A 22
Darby's Clo. BH15—1E 21
Darby's La. BH17 & BH15—6F 9
(in two parts)
Dark La. BH23—1B 18
Dark La. BH25—1G 19
Darracott Rd. BH5—3B 26
Darwin Av. BH23—4F 15
Davis Field. BH25—2G 19
Davis Rd. BH12—2D 22
Dawkins Rd. BH23—3A 20
Dawkins Way. BH25—3H 19
Dawn Clo. BH10—3H 11
Daws Av. BH11—3F 11
Daylesford Clo. BH14—5H 11
Deacon Rd. BH11—6F 5
Dean Clo. BH15—4A 20
Dean Pk. Cres. BH1—3C 24
Dean Pk. Rd. BH1—3C 24
Deanscroft Rd. BH10—1B 12
Deans Rd. BH5—2C 26
Dean Swift Cres. BH14—1B 30
Dear Hay La. BH15—5D 20
Decies Rd. BH14—2A 22
De Courtenai Clo. BH11—6D 4
Deepdene La. BH11—6D 4
Dee Way. BH15—5C 20
De Haviland Clo. BH21—1G 3
De Havilland Way. BH23—2D 28
Delamere Gdns. BH10—2B 12
Delft M. BH23—6B 16
Delhi Clo. BH14—4C 22
Delhi Rd. BH9—2B 12
De Lisle Rd. BH3—6C 12
Dell Clo. BH18—1A 8
Dell, The. BH25—5D 18
Delph Rd. BH21—3E 3
Delta Clo. BH23—6E 17
De Mauley Rd. BH13—1D 30
De Montfort Rd. BH21—2F 3
Denby Rd. BH15—1H 21
Deneve Av. BH17—4E 9
Dene Wlk. BH22—2B 6

Denewood Rd. BH4—5G 23
Denham Clo. BH17—2F 9
Denham Dri. BH23—4A 18
Denison Rd. BH17—4D 8
Denmark La. BH15—4E 21
Denmark Rd. BH9—4C 12
Denmark Rd. BH15—4E 21
Denmead Rd. BH6—6D 14
Dennistoun Av. BH23—6C 16
Derby Rd. BH1—3F 25
De Redvers Rd. BH14—5B 22
Dereham Way. BH12—1E 23
Derwent Clo. BH9—2C 12
Derwentwater Rd. BH21—1E 3
Derweston Clo. BH9—1E 13
Devon Rd. BH15—2G 21
Devon Rd. BH23—5E 15
Diana Way. BH21—3A 2
Dibden Clo. BH9—2B 12
Dickens Rd. BH6—6E 15
Dilly La. BH25—5H 19
Dingle Rd. BH5—3B 26
Dingley Rd. BH15—1F 21
Diprose Rd. BH21—4A 2
Disraeli Rd. BH23—1B 28
Dogwood Rd. BH18—3A 8
Dolbery Rd. BH12—3C 10
Dolphin Av. BH10—6A 6
Dolphin Pl. BH25—6H 19
Dolphin Shopping Centre. BH15—4E 21
Dominion Rd. BH11—1D 10
Donnelly Rd. BH6—2F 27
Donnington Dri. BH23—6F 17
Donoughmore Rd. BH1—3G 25
Dorchester Gdns. BH15—2G 21
Dorchester Rd. BH15—1E 21
Dornie Rd. BH13—2D 30
Dorset Lake Av. BH14—1B 30
Dorset Rd. BH4—2G 23
Dorset Rd. BH23—5C 16
Dorset Way. BH17 & BH12—5H 9 to 3A 10
Douglas Av. BH23—1F 27
Douglas Gdns. BH12—2D 22
Douglas Rd. BH6—3E 27
Douglas Rd. BH12—2D 22
Dover Clo. BH13—4F 23
Dover Rd. BH13—4F 23
Doveshill Cres. BH10—2A 12
Doveshill Gdns. BH10—2A 12
Dowlands Clo. BH10—1A 12
Dowlands Rd. BH10—1H 11
Downey Clo. BH11—3E 11
Downton Clo. BH8—1F 13
Doyne Rd. BH14—3D 22
Drake Clo. BH23—1D 28
Drake Clo. BH25—2G 19
Drake Rd. BH15—6D 20
Draper Rd. BH11—1F 11
Draper Rd. BH23—5C 16
Draycott Rd. BH10—2A 12
Dreswick Clo. BH23—1E 15
Drew Clo. BH12—5H 11
Drive, The. BH12—2B 22
Droxford Rd. BH6—1C 26
Druids Clo. BH22—1A 6
Druitt Rd. BH23—5C 16
Drummond Rd. BH1—2F 25
Drury Rd. BH4—5G 23
Ducking Stool La. BH23—1H 27
Duck La. BH11—1E 11
Dudley Gdns. BH10—6A 6
Dudley Rd. BH10—6A 6
Dudmoor Farm Rd. BH23—1F 15
Dudsbury Gdns. BH22—3B 6
Dudsbury Rd. BH22—2A 6
Dukes Dri. BH11—5D 4
Dukes Field. BH23—3D 14
Dulsie Rd. BH3—1H 23
Dunbar Cres. BH23—3B 18
Dunbar Rd. BH3—1B 24
Duncliff Rd. BH6—3G 27

Dundas Rd. BH17—5F 9
Dunedin Gro. BH23—6G 17
Dunford Clo. BH25—4F 19
Dunford Rd. BH12—2C 22
Dunkeld Rd. BH3—6A 12
Dunlin Clo. BH23—2E 29
Dunstans La. BH15—1H 21
Dunyeats Rd. BH18—6C 2
Durdells Av. BH11—5F 5
Durdells Gdns. BH11—6F 5
Durland Clo. BH25—3H 19
Durley Chine. BH2—5A 24
Durley Chine Ct. BH2—5A 24
Durley Chine Rd. BH2—4A 24
Durley Chine Rd. S. BH2—5A 24
Durley Gdns. BH2—5A 24
Durley Prom. BH4—6H 23
Durley Rd. BH2—5A 24
Durley Rd. S. BH2—5A 24
Durlston Cres. BH23—1D 14
Durlston Rd. BH14—5B 22
Durrant Rd. BH2—3B 24
Durrant Rd. BH14—4B 22
Durrington Pl. BH7—6B 14
Durrington Rd. BH7—6B 14

Eagle Rd. BH12—3F 23
Earle Rd. BH4—6D 23
Earlham Dri. BH14—3B 22
Earlsdon Way. BH23—4B 18
East Av. BH3—1H 23
East Av. BH25—6E 19
E. Cliff Prom. BH1—5C 24
E. Cliff Way. BH23—6G 17
East Clo. BH25—5F 19
Eastcott Clo. BH7—5A 14
Easter Rd. BH9—3D 12
E. Howe La. BH10—1H 11
Eastlake Av. BH12—1A 22
E. Overcliff Dri. BH1—5D 24
E. Quay Rd. BH15—6D 20
East St. BH15—5E 21
East Way. BH8—4E 13
East Way. BH21—6A 2
Eaton Rd. BH13—5F 23
Ebor Rd. BH12—1C 22
Edgarton Rd. BH17—2E 9
Edgehill Rd. BH9—5B 12
Edifred Rd. BH9—5B 12
Edmunds Clo. BH25—4H 19
Edward Rd. BH11—2G 11
Edward Rd. BH14—2C 22
Edward Rd. BH23—5E 15
Edwina Dri. BH17—3D 8
Egdon Dri. BH21—3F 3
Egerton Gdns. BH8—1G 25
Egerton Rd. BH23—1D 28
Elderberry La. BH23—4F 15
Eldon Av. BH25—4G 19
Eldon Clo. BH25—5G 19
Eldon Pl. BH4—4G 23
Eldon Rd. BH9—4A 12
Eleanor Dri. BH11—6C 4
Elgar Rd. BH10—1A 12
Elgin Rd. BH3—6A 12
Elgin Rd. BH4—1A 24
Elise Clo. BH7—5B 14
Elizabeth Rd. BH23—5F 15
Elizabeth Gdns. BH23—5G 17
Elizabeth Rd. BH15—4E 21
Ellesfield Dri. BH22—1A 22
Elliott Rd. BH11—2D 10
Elm Av. BH23—4E 15
Elm Av. BH25—2H 19
Elmes Rd. BH9—3B 12
Elmgate Dri. BH7—5A 14
Elmhurst Rd. BH11—6F 5
Elms Av. BH14—6H 21
Elms Clo. BH14—6A 22
Elms Gdns. BH4—2H 23
Elmstead Rd. BH13—1E 31
Elmsway. BH6—3E 27
Elm Tree Wlk. BH22—2B 6

Elmwood Way. BH23—6B 18
Elphinstone Rd. BH23—4C 18
Eltham Clo. BH7—5C 14
Elwyn Rd. BH1—2E 24
Emerson Clo. BH15—5E 21
Emerson Rd. BH15—5E 21
Emily Clo. BH23—4G 15
Encombe Clo. BH12—5E 11
Endfield Clo. BH23—4F 15
Endfield Rd. BH9—4E 13
Endfield Rd. BH23—4E 15
Enfield Av. BH15—1G 21
Enfield Cres. BH15—1G 21
Enfield Rd. BH9—3C 12
Enfield Rd. BH15—1F 21
Englands Way. BH11—1D 10
Ensbury Av. BH10—3H 11
Ensbury Clo. BH10—4A 12
Ensbury Pk. Rd. BH9—3B 12
Ericksen Rd. BH11—1G 11
Erpingham Rd. BH12—2F 23
Esmonde Way. BH17—5G 9
Esplanade. BH15—6D 20
Essex Av. BH23—3F 15
Ettrick Rd. BH13—1E 31
Evans Clo. BH11—3E 11
Evelyn Rd. BH9—3C 12
Everest Rd. BH23—5C 16
Evering Av. BH12—4B 10
Evering Gdns. BH12—4C 10
Evershot Rd. BH8—6G 13
Evesham Clo. BH7—5B 14
Exbury Dri. BH11—6E 5
Excelsior Rd. BH14—4B 22
Exeter Cres. BH2—4B 24
Exeter La. BH2—4C 24
Exeter Pk. Rd. BH2—5C 24
Exeter Rd. BH2—4B 24
Exton Rd. BH6—6D 14

Fairfield. BH23—6H 15
Fairfield Clo. BH23—6H 15
Fairfield Rd. BH25—5F 19
Fairmile Rd. BH23—3F to 6G 15
Fairview Cres. BH18—6C 2
Fairview Rd. BH18—6C 2
Fairview Rd. BH18—6C 2
Fairway Rd. BH23—1F 27
Fairway Rd. BH14—1C 30
Falcon Dri. BH23—2E 29
Falconer Dri. BH15—3A 20
Falkland Sq. BH15—5E 21
Fancy Rd. BH17—4A 10
Farcroft Rd. BH12—2A 22
Farewell Clo. BH23—2A 16
Farm Dene Clo. BH23—5H 17
Farm La. BH25—6H 19
Farm La. N. BH25—5H 19
Farnham Rd. BH12—6F 11
Farwell Rd. BH12—2B 10
Fawcett Rd. BH25—2H 19
Fawley Grn. BH8—2G 13
Felton Cres. BH23—4B 18
Felton Rd. BH15—2G 21
Fenton Rd. BH6—1C 26
Fern Barrow. BH12—5G 11
Fern Clo. BH23—3A 16
Ferncroft Gdns. BH10—6A 6
Ferncroft Rd. BH10—6A 6
Ferndale. BH25—1H 19
Ferndown Rd. BH11—2F 11
Fernheath Clo. BH11—2F 11
Fernheath Rd. BH11—2F 11
Fernhill Clo. BH17—3H 9
Fernhill La. BH25—1H 19
Fernhill Rd. BH25—1H 19
Fernside Av. BH14—3G 21
Fernside Rd. BH9—5A 12
Fernside Rd. BH15—2F 21
Ferris Av. BH8—2F 13
Ferris Clo. BH8—2F 13
Ferris Pl. BH8—2F 13
Ferry Rd. BH6—4F 27
Ferry Rd. BH15—6D 20
Ferry Way. BH13—6A 30

Feversham Av. BH8—4G 13
Field Pl. BH25—5E 19
Field Way. BH21—3A 2
Fieldway. BH23—4H 17
Finchfield Av. BH11—5E 5
Firbank Rd. BH9—5E 13
Firmain Rd. BH12—4D 10
Firs Glen Rd. BH9—5A 12
Firshill. BH23—4A 18
Firs La. BH14—1B 30
First Marine Av. BH25—6H 19
Fir Tree La. BH23—3H 17
Fir Vale Rd. BH1—4C 24
Fishermans Av. BH6—3C 26
Fishermans Bank. BH23—2C 28
Fishermans Rd. BH15—6E 21
Fitzharris Av. BH9—6C 12
Fitzmaurice Rd. BH23—5E 15
Fitzpain Clo. BH22—1A 6
Fitzpain Rd. BH22—1A 6
Fitzwilliam Clo. BH11—6D 4
Flag Head Chine. BH13—3D 30
Flaghead Rd. BH13—2D 30
Flambard Av. BH23—4A 18
Flambard Rd. BH14—4B 22
Fleetsbridge Retail Pk. BH17—1D 20
Fleets La. BH15—6D 8
Fletcher Clo. BH10—1A 12
Fletcher Rd. BH10—1A 12
Floral Farm. BH21—1H 3
Florence Rd. BH5—3H 25
Florence Rd. BH14—2C 22
Fontmell Rd. BH18—3D 8
Footners La. BH23—3A 16
Foreland Clo. BH23—1D 14
Forest Clo. BH23—4H 17
Forest Rise. BH23—3H 17
Forest Rd. BH13—6F 23
Forest View Clo. BH9—2D 12
Forest View Dri. BH9—2D 12
Forest Way. BH23—3G 17
Forsyth Gdns. BH10—3H 11
Fortescue Rd. BH3—1C 24
Fortescue Rd. BH12—6C 10
Foxcote Gdns. BH25—2G 19
Foxholes Rd. BH6—3F 27
Foxholes Rd. BH15—1G 21
Foxwood Av. BH23—1C 28
Frampton Rd. BH9—5E 13
Frances Rd. BH1—3E 25
Francis Av. BH11—1C 10
Francis Rd. BH12—2D 22
Frankland Cres. BH14—4D 22
Franklin Rd. BH9—2D 12
Frankston Rd. BH6—2C 26
Franks Way. BH14—6A 10
Fraser Rd. BH12—4E 11
Freda Rd. BH23—1F 27
Frederica Rd. BH9—5B 12
French Rd. BH17—4D 8
Frensham Clo. BH10—2B 12
Freshwater Dri. BH15—4A 20
Freshwater Rd. BH23—1G 29
Friars Rd. BH23—1F 29
Friars Wlk. BH25—5H 19
Fritham Gdns. BH8—2F 13
Frobisher Av. BH12—4F 11
Frobisher Clo. BH23—1D 28
Frost Rd. BH11—1E 11
Fryers Clo. BH10—5G 5
Fulmar Rd. BH23—2E 29
Fulwood Av. BH11—5E 5
Furnell Rd. BH15—6E 21
Furze Bank La. BH10—3H 11
Furzebrook Clo. BH17—2F 9
Furze Croft. BH25—3H 19
Furze Hill Dri. BH14—6C 22

Gainsborough Rd. BH7—6H 13
Gallows Dri. BH22—1A 6
Galton Av. BH23—1F 27
Garden Clo. BH25—3H 19

Gardens Cres. BH14—1B 30
Gardens Rd. BH14—1B 30
Gardner Rd. BH23—5E 15
Garfield Av. BH1—1F 25
Garland Rd. BH15—3F 21
Garsdale Clo. BH11—6D 4
Garth Rd. BH9—4C 12
Gaydon Rise. BH11—6D 4
Geneva Rd. BH6—2D 26
Georgian Way. BH10—1B 12
Georgina Clo. BH12—5H 11
Gerald Rd. BH3—6D 12
Germaine Clo. BH12—5B 18
Gervis Cres. BH14—3A 22
Gervis Pl. BH1—4C 24
Gervis Rd. BH1—4D 24
Gibson Rd. BH17—6F 9
Gilbert Rd. BH8—1F 25
Gillam Rd. BH10—6A 6
Gillingham Clo. BH9—1E 13
Gladdis Rd. BH11—1E 11
Gladelands Clo. BH18—1A 8
Gladelands Way. BH18—1A 8
(in two parts)
Gladstone Clo. BH23—1B 28
Gladstone Rd. BH7—2H 25
Gladstone Rd. BH12—2B 22
Gladstone Rd. W. BH1—2H 25
Glams Av. BH10—6A 6
Gleadowe Av. BH23—6F 15
Glenair Av. BH11—4H 21
Glenair Cres. BH14—4H 21
Glenair Rd. BH11—4H 21
Glenavon Rd. BH23—4B 18
Glen Clo. BH25—5E 19
Glencoe Rd. BH7—6H 13
Glencoe Rd. BH12—1C 22
Glendale Clo. BH23—5B 18
Glendale Rd. BH6—3G 27
Glendon Av. BH10—5H 5
Glen Dri. BH25—5D 18
Gleneagles Av. BH14—5C 22
Glenferness Av. BH4 & BH3
—2H 23 to 6A 12
Glen Fern Rd. BH1—4C 24
Glengariff Rd. BH14—4C 22
Glengarry Way. BH23—1F 29
Glenmeadows Dri. BH10—6G 5
Glenmoor Clo. BH10—4A 12
Glenmoor Rd. BH9—2A 12
Glen Mt. Dri. BH14—2A 22
Glen Rd. BH5—2H 25
Glen Rd. BH14—2A 22
Glenroyd Gdns. BH6—2E 27
Glenside. BH25—6D 18
Glenville Clo. BH23—3C 18
Glenville Rd. BH10—3H 11
Glenville Rd. BH23—3C 18
Glissons. BH22—1F 5
Globe La. BH15—5E 21
Gloucester Rd. BH7—1H 25
Gloucester Rd. BH12—2D 22
Godmanston Clo. BH17—3H 9
Godshill Clo. BH8—2F 13
Goldfinch Rd. BH17—4A 8
Golf Links Rd. BH18—6C 2
Golf Links Rd. BH22—1B 6
Good Rd. BH12—6C 10
Gordon Rd. BH1—3G 25
Gordon Rd. BH12—2F 23
Gordon Rd. BH23—4C 18
Gordon Rd. S. BH12—2F 23
Gordon Way. BH23—4A 16
Gore Rd. BH25—3E 19
Gorey Rd. BH12—3C 10
Gorleston Rd. BH12—2E 23
Gorse Hill Clo. BH15—2G 21
Gorse Hill Rd. BH15—2G 21
Gort Rd. BH11—1G 11
Gort Rd. BH17—4C 8
Gosling Clo. BH17—5G 9
Gough Cres. BH17—3D 8

Grafton Clo. BH23—1B 28
Grafton Rd. BH3—1C 24
Granby Rd. BH9—6D 6
Grand Av. BH6—3C 26
Grande Pde. BH10—5H 5
Grange Gdns. BH12—5D 10
Grange Rd. BH6—4D 26
Grange Rd. BH18—1C 8
Grange Rd. BH23—6E 17
Grantham Rd. BH1—2G 25
Grantley Rd. BH5—3H 25
Grants Av. BH1—1G 25
Grants Clo. BH1—1G 25
Granville Rd. BH5—2B 26
Granville Rd. BH12—2B 22
Grasmere Clo. BH23—2E 15
Grasmere Rd. BH5—3A 26
Grasmere Rd. BH13—6A 30
Gravel Hill. BH17 & BH21
—3E 9 to 2E 3
Gray Clo. BH17—5G 9
Graycot Clo. BH10—5H 5
Greaves Clo. BH10—2H 11
Grebe Clo. BH17—5A 8
Grebe Clo. BH23—1E 29
Green Acre. BH25—5H 19
Greenacres Clo. BH10—4B 6
Green Clo. BH15—6E 21
Greenfield Rd. BH15—6G 9
Greenfinch Clo. BH17—3B 8
Green Gdns. BH15—6E 21
Greenhayes. BH17—3D 8
Green La. BH10—1H 11
Green La. BH22—1F 5
Green Rd. BH9—5C 12
Green Rd. BH15—5E 21
Greensleeves Av. BH18—5D 2
Greenways. BH23—5B 18
Greenways Av. BH8—1F 13
Greenwood Av. BH14—6G 22
Greenwood Rd. BH9—4B 12
Grenfell Rd. BH9—1C 12
Gresham Rd. BH9—1C 12
Greystoke Av. BH11—5E 5
Grosvenor Gdns. BH1—3G 25
Grosvenor Rd. BH4—4H 23
Groveley Rd. BH4—5G 23
Groveley Rd. BH23—6C 16
Grovely Av. BH5—3A 26
Grove Rd. BH1—4D 24
Grove Rd. BH12—1A 22
Grove Rd. BH25—6H 19
Grove Rd. E. BH23—5G 15
Grove Rd. W. BH23—5F 15
Grove, The. BH9—2C 12
Grove, The. BH23—4E 15
Guernsey Rd. BH12—4C 10
Guest Av. BH12—1E 23
Guest Clo. BH12—1F 23
Guild Hill BH6—3E 27
Gulliver Clo. BH14—1B 30
Gunville Cres. BH9—2E 13
Gurney Rd. BH21—4A 2
Gussage Rd. BH12—5E 11
Gwynne Rd. BH12—2D 22

Haarlem M. BH23—6B 16
Hadden Rd. BH8—5G 13
Hadley Way. BH18—1A 8
Hadow Rd. BH10—2H 11
Hadrian Clo. BH22—1A 6
Hadrian Way. BH21—3A 2
Hahnemann Rd. BH2—5A 24
Haig Av. BH13—6D 22
Halewood Way. BH23—5F 15
Halifax Way. BH23—6E 17
Hall Rd. BH11—1E 11
Halstock Cres. BH17—3F 9
Halter Path. BH15—4A 20
Hambledon Gdns. BH6—1C 26
Hambledon Rd. BH7 & BH8
—6B 14
Hamble Rd. BH15—6H 9

Hamilton Clo. BH1—2G 25
Hamilton Clo. BH15—5A 20
Hamilton Clo. BH23—2D 28
Hamilton Cres. BH15—5A 20
Hamilton Rd. BH1—2G 25
Hamilton Rd. BH15—5A 20
Hamilton Rd. BH21—6A 2
Hamilton Way. BH25—3G 19
Ham La. BH22—1E 5
Hampden La. BH6—2C 26
Hampreston Rd. BH22—1F 5
Hampshire Clo. BH23—3F 15
Hanham Rd. BH21—5A 2
Hankinson Rd. BH9—5C 12
Hannington Pl. BH7—2B 26
Hannington Rd. BH7—2A 26
Harbeck Rd. BH8—1F 13
Harbour Clo. BH13—3D 30
Harbour Cres. BH23—2C 28
Harbour Hill Cres. BH15—2F 21
Harbour Hill Rd. BH15—2F 21
Harbour Rd. BH6—4G 27
Harbour View Clo. BH14—2H 21
Harbour View Rd. BH14—2H 21
Harcombe Clo. BH17—2F 9
Harcourt Rd. BH5—2B 26
Hardy Clo. BH25—2G 19
Hardy Rd. BH14—3C 22
Hares Grn. BH7—5B 14
Harewood Av. BH7—5H 13
Harewood Cres. BH7—5H 13
Harewood Gdns. BH7—6A 14
Harewood Pl. BH7—1B 26
Harford Rd. BH12—5B 10
Harkwood Dri. BH15—3A 20
Harland Rd. BH6—3G 27
Harrier Dri. BH21—1H 3
Harriers Clo. BH23—5H 17
Harrison Av. BH1—1G 25
Harrison Clo. BH23—6H 17
Harting Rd. BH6—6D 14
Harvey Rd. BH5—2A 26
Harvey Rd. BH21—3G & 2G 3
Haskells Rd. BH12—6A 10
Haslemere Av. BH23—4B 18
Haslemere Pl. BH23—4B 18
Hasler Rd. BH17—3E 9
Hastings Rd. BH8—3H 13
Hastings Rd. BH17—3G 8
Hatch Pond Rd. BH17—5D 8
Hatfield Ct. BH25—1F 19
Hatfield Gdns. BH8—5B 14
Hathaway Rd. BH6—3E 27
Hatherden Av. BH14—2H 21
Havelock Rd. BH12—2F 23
Havelock Way. BH23—3H 17
Haven Rd. BH13—3C 30 to 1E 31
Haverstock Rd. BH6—2D 12
Haviland M. BH1—2H 25
Haviland Rd. BH7—2H 25
Hawden Rd. BH11—4F 11
Hawkchurch Gdns. BH17—2G 9
Hawker Clo. BH21—4A 2
Hawkins Rd. BH12—4E 11
Hawkwood Rd. BH5—2B 26
Haworth Clo. BH23—4G 15
Hawthorn Dri. BH17—4B 8
Hawthorn Rd. BH9—4B 12
Hawthorn Rd. BH23
—5C to 1C 16
Hawthorns, The. BH23—1D 28
Haydon Rd. BH13—6G 23
Hayes Av. BH7—1G 25
Haymoor Rd. BH15—4E 11
Haynes Av. BH15—3E 21
Hazebury Rd. BH17—6C 8
Hazel Clo. BH23—4G 17
Hazell Av. BH10—3G 11
Hazelton Clo. BH7—5B 14
Hazelwood Av. BH25—1G 19
Heads Farm Clo. BH10—6B 6
Heads La. BH10—6B 6
Headswell Av. BH10—1B 12

Headswell Cres. BH10—1B 12
Headswell Gdns. BH10—6B 6
Heanor Clo. BH10—2H 11
Heath Av. BH15—1E 21
Heathcote Rd. BH5—3H 25
Heather Bank Rd. BH4—4H 23
Heather Clo. BH8—1F 13
Heather Clo. BH21—5A 2
Heather Clo. BH23—3C 18
Heatherlea Rd. BH6—3D 26
Heather Rd. BH10—2H 11
Heather View Rd. BH12—6E 11
Heathfield Av. BH12—5F 11
Heathlands Av. BH22—1A 6
Heathlands Clo. BH23—2A 16
Heath Rd. BH23—4C 18
Heathwood Av. BH25—5F 19
Heathwood Rd. BH9—5B 12
Heathy Clo. BH25—5G 19
Heaton Rd. BH10—3G 11
Heavytree Rd. BH14—3A 22
Heckford Rd. BH15—3E 21
Helyar Rd. BH8—3A 14
Henbury Clo. BH17—3H 9
Hendford Gdns. BH10—3A 12
Hendford Rd. BH10—3A 12
Hengistbury Rd. BH6—3F 27
Hengistbury Rd. BH25—5F 19
Hengist Rd. BH1—4C 24
Henley Gdns. BH7—6A 14
Hennings Pk. Rd. BH15—2F 21
Henville Rd. BH8—1E 25
Herbert Av. BH12
—4B 10 to 1E 22
Herberton Rd. BH6—2C 26
Herbert Rd. BH4—5G 23
Herbert Rd. BH25—2H 19
Hermitage Rd. BH14—1H 21
Herm Rd. BH12—4C 10
Heron Ct. Rd. BH9 & BH3—6D 12
Herstone Clo. BH17—3G 9
Hestan Clo. BH23—1D 14
Hewitt Rd. BH15—3A 20
Heysham Rd. BH18—1C 8
Heytesbury Rd. BH10—1D 26
Hibberd Way. BH10—4A 12
Highcliffe Corner. BH23—5C 18
Highcliffe Rd. BH23—5E 17
Higher Blandford Rd. BH21
—4A 2
Higher Merley La. BH21—2A 2
Highfield Clo. BH21—6A 2
Highfield Rd. BH9—3B 12
Highfield Rd. BH21—6A 2
High Howe Clo. BH11—1D 10
High Howe La. BH11—6D 4
Highland Av. BH23—4C 18
Highland Rd. BH14—2A 22
Highlands Cres. BH10—6H 5
Highlands Rd. BH25—5H 19
High Mead La. BH27—1H 3
Highmoor Clo. BH14—4B 22
Highmoor Clo. BH11—3F 11
Highmoor Rd. BH11—3F 11
Highmoor Rd. BH14—4B 22
Highmoor Rd. BH21—6A 2
High Pk. Rd. BH18—6A 2
High St. Christchurch, BH23
—1H 27
High St. N. BH15—4E 21
High St. Poole, BH15—6D 20
Hightrees Av. BH8—4H 13
Highview Clo. BH23—4E 15
Highview Gdns. BH12—6B 10
High Way. BH14—2B 8
Highwood Rd. BH14—3D 22
Hilary Rd. BH17—3D 8
Hilda Rd. BH12—6D 10
Hiley Rd. BH15—1E 21
Hillary Rd. BH23—5C 16
Hillbourne Rd. BH17—3C 8
Hillbrow Rd. BH6—1B 26
Hillcrest Clo. BH9—2D 12
Hillcrest Rd. BH9—2C 12

Hillcrest Rd. BH12—2A 22
Hill La. BH23—3C 16 to 1F 17
Hillman Rd. BH14—2C 22
Hillside Dri. BH23—1D 14
Hillside Rd. BH12—4E 11
Hill St. BH15—5D 20
Hill Ter. BH21—1H 3
Hilltop Rd. BH21—5A 2
Hillview Rd. BH10—1A 12
Hilton Clo. BH15—1H 21
Hinchcliffe Clo. BH15—5B 20
Hinchcliffe Rd. BH15—5A 20
Hinton Rd. BH1—4C 24
Hinton Wood Av. BH23—3A 18
Hinton Wood La. BH23—2H 17
Hobart Rd. BH25—3H 19
Hobbs Rd. BH12—5B 10
Hoburne Gdns. BH23—4G 17
Hoburne La. BH23—3G 17
Hodges Clo. BH17—5G 9
Hogue Av. BH10—6A 6
Holbury Clo. BH6—2G 13
Holdenhurst Av. BH7—1C 26
Holdenhurst Rd. BH8
—4D 24 to 1G 25
(Bournemouth centre)
Holdenhurst Rd. BH8—2A 14
(Holdenhurst)
Holes Bay Rd. BH17 & BH15
—1C 20 to 4E 21
Holland Way. BH18—6A 2
Holloway Av. BH11—6E 5
Holly Gdns. BH23—3B 16
Holly Grn. Rise. BH11—6D 4
Holly Hedge La. BH17—5E 9
Holly La. BH23—3D 18
Holme Rd. BH23—5C 18
Holmfield Av. BH7—5C 14
Holmhurst Av. BH23—4A 18
Holnest Rd. BH17—4E 9
Holt Rd. BH12—1E 23
Holworth Clo. BH11—1D 10
Holywell Clo. BH17—2F 9
Home Rd. BH11—5G 5
Homeside Rd. BH9—3D 12
Honeybourne Cres. BH6—3G 27
Honeysuckle La. BH17—4B 8
Honeysuckle Way. BH23—5F 17
Hood Clo. BH10—4G 11
Hood Cres. BH10—4G 11
Hooke Clo. BH17—3H 9
Hopkins Clo. BH8—2D 12
Horace Rd. BH5—3G 25
Horning Rd. BH12—2E 23
Horsa Clo. BH6—3E 27
Horsa Rd. BH6—3E 27
Horseshoe, The. BH13—5B 30
Horsham Av. BH10—5H 5
Horton Clo. BH9—1F 13
Hosker Rd. BH5—2C 26
Houlton Rd. BH15—3F 21
Hounslow Clo. BH15—5A 20
Howard Clo. BH23—1D 28
Howard Rd. BH8—6E 13
Howe Clo. BH23—1D 28
Howe Clo. BH25—2G 19
Howeth Clo. BH10—2A 12
Howeth Rd. BH10—1H 11
Howton Clo. BH10—5H 5
Howton Rd. BH10—5H 5
Hoxley Rd. BH10—5H 5
Hoyal Rd. BH15—4A 20
Hudson Clo. BH12—3B 10
Hull Cres. BH11—6D 4
Hull Rd. BH11—6D 4
Hull Way. BH11—1D 10
Humphrey's Bri. BH25—2F 19
Hungerford Rd. BH8—2F 13
Hunter Clo. BH23—6E 17
Huntfield Rd. BH9—2E 13
Huntingdon Dri. BH21—2F 3
Huntingdon Gdns. BH23—3G 15
Huntly Rd. BH3—1H 23
Hunt Rd. BH15—3G 21

Hunt Rd. BH23—5C 16
Huntvale Rd. BH9—2E 13
Hurn Rd. BH23—1D 14
Hurn Way. BH23—4D 14
Hursley Clo. BH7—5C 14
Hurstbourne Av. BH23—3A 18
Hurst Clo. BH23—3D 18
Hurstdene Rd. BH8—2F 13
Hurst Hill. BH14—1B 30
Hyacinth Clo. BH17—4A 8
Hyde Rd. BH10—6H 5
Hynesbury Rd. BH23—1F 29
Hythe Rd. BH15—6H 9

Ibbertson Clo. BH8—3A 14
Ibbertson Rd. BH8—3A 14
Ibbertson Way. BH8—3A 14
Ibbett Rd. BH10—2H 11
Ibsley Clo. BH8—1F 25
Iddesleigh Rd. BH3—6C 12
Iford Clo. BH6—1F 27
Iford Gdns. BH7—6D 14
Iford La. BH6—6D 14 to 2F 27
Imber Dri. BH23—5B 18
Imbrecourt. BH13—2D 30
Inglesham Way. BH23—3A 20
Inglewood Av. BH8—4H 13
Ingworth Rd. BH12—2F 23
Insley Cres. BH18—5A 2
Inveravon. BH23—2D 28
Inverclyde Rd. BH14—3B 22
Inverleigh Rd. BH6—1D 26
Inverness Rd. BH13—2D 30
Ipswich Rd. BH12 & BH4—3G 23
Iris Rd. BH9—4B 12
Irvine Way. BH23—5C 16
Irving Rd. BH6—3D 26
Island View. BH25—6E 19
Island View Av. BH23—1F 29
Island View Ct. BH25—5H 19
Island View Rd. BH25—6E 19
Ivamy Pl. BH11—3E 11
Ivor Rd. BH15—6C 20
Ivy Rd. BH21—3E 3
Iwerne Clo. BH9—1E 13

Jackson Rd. BH12—1C 22
Jacobean Clo. BH23—4C 18
Jacqueline Rd. BH12—6B 10
Jameson Rd. BH9—4B 12
James Rd. BH12—2F 23
Jays Ct. BH23—5C 18
Jefferson Av. BH1—1G 25
Jellicoe Dri. BH23—1D 28
Jennings Rd. BH14—5B 22
Jephcote Rd. BH11—1E 11
Jersey Clo. BH12—3C 10
Jersey Rd. BH12—3C 10
Jesmond Av. BH23—5B 18
Jessop Clo. BH10—1C 12
Jewell Rd. BH8—3A 14
Johnstone Rd. BH23—1C 28
Johnston Rd. BH15—6F 9
Jolliffe Av. BH15—3E 21
Jolliffe Rd. BH15—3E 21
Jowitt Dri. BH25—2G 19
Jubilee Cres. BH12—2C 22
Jubilee Gdns. BH10—3A 12
Jubilee Rd. BH12—2C 22
Jubilee Rd. BH21—4A 2
Julia Clo. BH23—5A 18
Julyan Av. BH12—5F 11
Jumpers Av. BH23—4E 15
Jumpers Rd. BH23—5F 15
Junction Rd. BH9—5C 12
Jupiter Way. BH23—3A 2
Justin Gdns. BH10—6B 6

Katherine Chance Clo. BH23
—2A 16
Katterns Clo. BH23—3E 15

Keeble Rd. BH10—5A 6
Keighley Av. BH18—3B 8
Keith Rd. BH3—1H 23
Kellaway Rd. BH17—5G 9
Kelly Gro. BH17—5G 9
Kemp Rd. BH9—5B 12
Kennard Ct. BH25—1G 19
Kennard Rd. BH25—1G 19
Kennart Rd. BH17—6C 8
Ken Rd. BH6—3E 27
Kensington Dri. BH2—3A 24
Kent Rd. BH12—1D 22
Kenyon Clo. BH15—6G 9
Kenyon Rd. BH15—6G 9
Kerley Rd. BH2—5B 24
Kestrel Dri. BH23—1E 29
Keswick Rd. BH5—3A 26
Keyes Clo. BH12—4E 11
Keyes Clo. BH23—1D 28
Keysworth Av. BH25—5G 19
Khyber Rd. BH12—2C 22
Kilmarnock Rd. BH9—4C 12
Kilmington Way. BH23—5A 18
Kimberley Clo. BH23—4F 15
Kimberley Rd. BH6—1C 26
Kimberley Rd. BH14—4A 22
Kimber Rd. BH11—1E 11
Kimmeridge Av. BH12—5B 10
King Edward Av. BH9—3C 12
King George Av. BH9—3C 12
King John Av. BH11—5C 4
Kingland Cres. BH15—5E 21
Kingland Rd. BH15—4E to 5F 21
King Richard Dri. BH11—6C 4
Kings Av. BH14—5C 22
King's Av. BH23—1F 27
Kingsbere Av. BH10—3G 11
Kingsbere Rd. BH15—2F 21
Kingsbourne Av. BH10—3A 12
Kingsbridge Rd. BH14—4B 22
Kings Cres. BH14—5D 22
Kingsley Av. BH6—3G 27
Kingsley Clo. BH6—3G 27
Kingsmill Rd. BH17—6F 9
Kings Pk. Central Dri. BH7
    —1G 25
Kings Pk. Dri. BH7
    —6G 13 & 1B 26
Kings Pk. Rd. BH7—1G 25
King's Rd. BH3—6D 12
Kingston Rd. BH10
    —4F 11 to 5H 5
Kingston Rd. BH15—3E 21
Kingsway Clo. BH23—4F 15
Kingswell Clo. BH10—3A 12
Kingswell Gdns. BH10—2G 11
Kingswell Gro. BH10—2G 11
Kingswell Rd. BH10—2G 11
Kinross Rd. BH3—1B 24
Kinson Av. BH15—6H 9
Kinson Gro. BH10—5H 5
Kinson Pk. Rd. BH10—4H 5
Kipling Rd. BH14—2A 22
Kirby Clo. BH15—1G 21
Kirby Way. BH6—3D 26
Kirkham Av. BH23—2A 16
Kirkway. BH18—1C 8
Kitchener Cres. BH17—4C 8
Kitscroft Rd. BH10—5H 5
Kiwi Clo. BH23—1D 14
Knapp Clo. BH23—5G 15
Knapp Mill Av. BH23—5G 15
Knighton Heath Clo. BH11
    —1D 10
Knighton Heath Rd. BH11
    10 10
Knighton La. BH21—4C 4
Knighton Rd. BH25—5F 19
Knights Rd. BH11—6D 4
Knightwood. BH25—6E 19
Knightwood Clo. BH23—5H 17
Knole Gdns. BH1—2F 25
Knole Rd. BH1—2F 25
Knowles Clo. BH23—5B 16

Knowlton Gdns. BH9—1D 12
Knowlton Rd. BH17—3G 9
Knyveton Rd. BH1—3E 25

Labrador Dri. BH15—6F 21
Laburnum Ho. BH10—1C 12
Lacey Cres. BH15—1A 22
Ladysmith Clo. BH23—6B 16
Lagado Clo. BH14—1C 30
Lagland St. BH15—5E 21
Lagoon Rd. BH14—1A 30
Laidlaw Clo. BH12—5G 11
Lake Av. BH15—6A 20
Lake Cres. BH15—4A 20
Lake Dri. BH15—5A 20
Lake Gro. Rd. BH25—1H 19
Lake Rd. BH11—5G 5
Lake Rd. BH15—6A 20
Lakeside Pines. BH25—1H 19
Lakeside Rd. BH13—6F 23
Lakewood Rd. BH23—4A 18
Lambs Clo. BH17—4D 8
Lambs Grn. La. BH21—1A 2
Lancaster Clo. BH18—6B 2
Lancaster Rd. BH23—6F 17
Lancaster Dri. BH18—5A 2
Lander Clo. BH15—6E 21
Landford Gdns. BH8—2G 13
Landford Way. BH8—3F 13
Landseer Rd. BH4—5H 23
Lane, The. BH8—2F 25
Langdon Rd. BH14—3C 22
Langley Rd. BH14—3E 23
Langley Rd. BH23—3H 17
Langside Av. BH12—5F 11
Langton Clo. BH25—4H 19
Langton Rd. BH7—2H 25
Lansdowne Cres. BH1—4D 24
Lansdowne Gdns. BH1—3D 24
Lansdowne Rd. BH1—1C 24
Lara Clo. BH8—1F 13
Larch Clo. BH17—4A 8
Lark Rd. BH23—1E 29
Larksfield Av. BH9—2E 13
Lascelles Rd. BH7—1B 26
Latch Farm Av. BH23—5G 15
Latimer Rd. BH9—5C 12
Latimers Clo. BH23—4A 18
Laurel Clo. BH23—4G 17
Laurel Dri. BH18—6D 2
Laurel Gdns. BH18—1D 8
Lavender Way. BH18—1A 8
Lavinia Rd. BH12—6B 10
Lawford Rd. BH9—1D 12
Lawns, The. BH23—5C 18
Lawrence Dri. BH13—6D 22
Lawson Rd. BH12—1B 22
Layard Dri. BH21—2F 3
Layton Rd. BH12—2C 22
Leamington Rd. BH9—6D 12
Leap Hill Rd. BH7—1B 26
Learoyd Rd. BH17—6F 9
Lea Way. BH11—5G 5
Lechlade Gdns. BH7—5B 14
Ledbury Rd. BH23—2C 28
Ledgard Clo. BH14—3B 22
Leedam Rd. BH10—6A 6
Lees Clo. BH23—1D 14
Leeson Rd. BH7—6H 13
Legion Clo. BH15—5A 20
Legion Rd. BH15—5A 20
Leicester Rd. BH13—3E 23
Leigh Rd. BH25—1H 19
Lentham Clo. BH17—4A 8
Le Patourel Clo. BH23—6B 16
Leslie Rd. BH9—5B 12
Leslie Rd. BH14—4H 21
Leven Av. BH4—2H 23
Leven Clo. BH4—3A 24
Levets La. BH15—5D 20
Lewesdon Dri. BH18—1B 8

Leybourne Av. BH10—6H 5
  (in two parts)
Leybourne Clo. BH10—6H 5
Leydene Av. BH8—4A 14
Leydene Clo. BH8—4H 13
Leyland Rd. BH12—3D 10
Leyside. BH23—6D 16
Library Rd. BH9—4B 12
Library Rd. BH12—2D 22
Lilliput Rd. BH14—1B 30
Lime Av. BH15—1G 21
Limited Rd. BH9—3D 12
Lincoln Av. BH1—1F 25
Lincoln Av. BH23—3F 15
Lincoln Rd. BH12—6C 10
Linden Clo. BH22—1A 6
Linden Rd. BH9—1C 12
Linden Rd. BH12—1B 22
Linden Rd. BH22—1A 6
Lindens, The. BH23—2B 16
Lindsay Rd. BH13—3E 23
Lineside. BH23—4A 16
Lingdale Rd. BH6—1D 26
Ling Rd. BH12—5A 10
Lingwood Av. BH23—1C 28
Link Rise. BH21—5A 2
Links Dri. BH23—4D 14
Linkside Av. BH8—4H 13
Links Rd. BH14—5C 22
Links View Av. BH14—6D 22
Linmead Dri. BH11—5A 4
Linnet Rd. BH17—4A 8
Linthorpe Rd. BH15—3G 21
Linwood Rd. BH9—6D 12
Lionheart Clo. BH11—6C 4
Lionheart Rd. BH11—6C 4
Littlecroft Av. BH9—2E 13
Lit. Croft Rd. BH12—1A 22
Littledown Av. BH7—6H 13
Littledown Dri. BH8—6H 13
Lit. Forest Rd. BH4—1A 24
Littlemead Clo. BH17—5B 8
Littlemoor Av. BH11—5F 5
Livingstone Rd. BH5—2B 26
Livingstone Rd. BH12—1B 22
Livingstone Rd. BH23—6B 16
Loch Rd. BH14—2D 22
Lockyers Rd. BH21—3A 2
Loders Clo. BH17—2E 9
Lodge Clo. BH14—3D 22
Lodge Rd. BH23—5E 15
Loewy Cres. BH17—5F 9
Lombard Av. BH6—2E 27
Lone Pine Dri. BH22—1B 6
Lone Pine Way. BH22—1C 6
Longbarrow Clo. BH8—4A 14
Longfield Dri. BH11—5F 5
Longfield Dri. BH22—3B 6
Longfleet Dri. BH17 & BH21
    —2F 9 to 3A 4
Longfleet Rd. BH15—4F 21
Longleat Gdns. BH25—2F 19
Longmeadow La. BH17—5A 8
Long Rd. BH10—6H 5
Longspee Rd. BH21—2F 3
Lonsdale Rd. BH14—5C 12
Loraine Av. BH23—6D 16
Lord Clo. BH17—5F 9
Lorne Pk. Rd. BH1—4D 24
Lwr. Blandford Rd. BH18
    —1C to 3D 8
Lwr. Golf Links Rd. BH18—6C 2
Lowther Gdns. BH8—2F 25
Lowther Rd. BH8—1D 24
Lucas Rd. BH12—1B 22
Lucerne Av. BH6—2D 26
Luckham Clo. BH9—3E 13
Luckham Gdns. BH9—2E 13
Luckham Pl. BH9—3E 13
Luckham Rd. BH9—3E 13
Luckham Rd. E. BH9—3E 13
Lulworth Av. BH15—6A 20
Lulworth Cres. BH15—6A 20
Luscombe Rd. BH14—5B 22

Luther Rd. BH9—5C 12
Lychett Minster & Upton
    By-Pass. BH16—6A 8
Lydford Gdns. BH11—2F 11
Lydford Rd. BH11—2F 11
Lydlinch Clo. BH22—2A 6
Lydwell Clo. BH11—5E 5
Lyell Rd. BH12—1C 22
Lyme Cres. BH23—5A 18
Lymington Rd. BH23
    —6G 17 to 5D 18
Lymington Rd. BH25—4H 19
Lyndhurst Rd. BH23
  (Somerford)—5E 17 to 1B 18
Lyndhurst Rd. BH23—1D 16
  (South Brockham)
Lynn Rd. BH17—4H 9
Lynric Clo. BH25—6H 19
Lynton Cres. BH23—1D 14
Lynwood Dri. BH21—3G 3
Lyon Rd. BH12—3D 10
Lysander Clo. BH23—6F 17
Lystra Rd. BH9—2D 12
Lytchett Dri. BH18—2B 8
Lytham Rd. BH18—2C 8
Lytton Rd. BH1—2E 25

Mabey Av. BH10—3A 12
Macandrew Rd. BH13—2E 30
Macaulay Rd. BH18—1C 8
McKinley Rd. BH4—5H 23
Maclaren Rd. BH9—2C 12
Maclean Rd. BH11—2E 11
McWilliam Clo. BH12—5H 11
McWilliam Rd. BH9—3C 12
Madeira Rd. BH1—3C 24
Madeira Rd. BH14—2C 22
Madeline Clo. BH12—6A 10
Madeline Cres. BH12—6A 10
Madison Av. BH1—1G 25
Magdalen La. BH23—1G 27
Magna Clo. BH11—5E 5
Magna Gdns. BH11—5E 5
Magna Rd. BH21 & BH11
    —2A 4 to 5E 5
Magnolia Clo. BH6—2G 27
Magnolia Ho. BH10—1C 12
Magpie Clo. BH8—2F 13
Mag's Barrow. BH22—1B 6
Maidment Clo. BH11—1D 10
Malan Clo. BH17—5F 9
Malcomb Clo. BH6—4G 27
Mallard Clo. BH8—4F 13
Mallard Clo. BH23—1E 29
Mallard Rd. BH8—4F 13
Mallory Clo. BH23—5D 16
Malmesbury Pk. Pl. BH8—2F 25
Malmesbury Pk. Rd. BH8
    —1D 24
Malvern Clo. BH9—2C 12
Malvern Rd. BH9—2C 12
Mandale Clo. BH11—1F 11
Mandale Rd. BH11—1E 11
Manning Av. BH23—4G 17
Mannings Heath Ind. Est. BH12
    —4A 10
Mannings Heath Rd. BH12
    —3A 10
Manor Av. BH12—4B 10
Manor Farm Clo. BH25—4G 19
Manor Farm Rd. BH10—4G 5
Manor Rd. BH1—4C 25
Manor Rd. BH23—1G 27
Manor Rd. BH25—2H 19
Mansfield Av. BH14—3B 22
Mansfield Clo. BH14—3B 22
Mansfield Clo. BH22—1A 22
Mansfield Rd. BH9—4B 12
Mansfield Rd. BH14—3B 22
Manton Rd. BH15—4A 20
Maple Clo. BH23—6B 18
Maple Rd. BH9—5B 12
Maple Rd. BH15—4F 21

Mapperton Clo. BH17—3H 9
Marabout Clo. BH23—6B 16
Marchwood Rd. BH10—1H 11
Marchwood Rd. BH14—6A 22
Marianne Rd. BH12—5H 11
Marina Clo. BH5—4G 25
Marina Dri. BH14—6A 22
Marina, The. BH5—4G 25
Marina View. BH23—2G 27
Marine Dri. BH25—6F 19
Marine Dri. E. BH25—6G 19
Marine Dri. W. BH25—6E 19
Marine Rd. BH6—4D 26
Market Clo. BH15—5D 20
Market St. BH15—6D 20
Markham Av. BH10—4A 6
Markham Rd. BH10—4A 6
Markham Rd. BH9—5C 12
Marks Rd. BH9—2C 12
Marlborough Rd. BH4—4H 23
Marlborough Rd. BH14—3B 22
Marley Av. BH25—1G 19
Marley Clo. BH25—1G 19
Marline Rd. BH12—1D 22
Marlott Rd. BH15—2E 20
Marlow Dri. BH23—2E 15
Marlpit Rd. BH23—4D 16
Marmion Grn. BH23—6D 16
Marnhull Rd. BH15—3F 21
Marpet Clo. BH11—5E 5
Marquis Way. BH11—6C 4
Marryat Ct. BH23—5C 18
Marryat Rd. BH25—2G 19
Marshal Rd. BH17—4D 8
Marsh La. BH23—3F & 3G 15
  (Fairmile)
Marsh La. BH23—1B 28
  (Purewell)
Marshwood Av. BH17—2G 9
Marston Gro. BH23—4A 18
Marston Rd. BH15—5D 20
Martello Clo. BH13—2E 31
Martello Rd. BH13—6D 22
Martello Rd. S. BH13—1E 31
Martin Clo. BH17—5B 8
Martins Hill Clo. BH23—4A 16
Martins Hill La. BH23—4A 16
Marwell Clo. BH7—6A 14
Maundeville Cres. BH23—5E 15
Maundeville Rd. BH23—5E 15
Maureen Clo. BH12—5B 10
Maurice Rd. BH8—5F 13
Mavis Rd. BH9—4E 13
Maxwell Rd. BH9—5C 12
Maxwell Rd. BH13—2E 31
Maxwell Rd. BH18—2A 8
Mayfair Gdns. BH11—6F 5
Mayfield Av. BH14—4D 22
Mayfield Pk. BH21—3A 2
Mayfield Rd. BH9—3C 12
Mayford Rd. BH12—6G 11
May Gdns. BH11—1D 10
Mead Clo. BH18—3C 8
Meadow Clo. BH22—2A 6
Meadow Ct. Clo. BH9—2C 12
Meadow Land. BH23—1C 28
Meadow Rise. BH18—5A 2
Meadowsweet Rd. BH17—4A 8
Meadow, The. BH25—5D 18
Meadow View Rd. BH11—1D 10
Meadow Way. BH25—6H 19
Meadway, The. BH23—3H 17
Medina Way. BH23—2G 27
Medlar Clo. BH23—4B 16
Melbourne Rd. BH8—1F 25
Melbourne Rd. BH23—4E 15
Melbury Av. BH12—5D 10
Mellstock Rd. BH15—2E 21
Melville Rd. BH9—5B 12
Mentone Rd. BH14—4H 21
Meon Rd. BH7—1B 26
Meredith Clo. BH23—6B 16
Meriden Clo. BH13—2E 31
Meridians, The. BH23—1F 27

Merlewood Clo. BH2—2B 24
Merley Dri. BH23—5B 18
Merley Gdns. BH21—2E 3
Merley Ho. La. BH21—1D 2
Merley La. BH21—2E 3
Merley Pk. Rd. BH21
    —2A 2 to 2E 3
Merley Ways. BH21—1E 3
Merlin Way. BH23—2E 29
Merriefield Av. BH18—5D 2
Merriefield Clo. BH18—5D 2
Merriefield Dri. BH18—5D 2
Merrivale Av. BH6—2E 27
Merrow Av. BH12—6G 11
Merryfield La. BH10—1H 11
Methuen Clo. BH8—2E 25
Methuen Rd. BH8—2E 25
Methuen Rd. BH17—3D 8
Meyrick Pk. Cres. BH3—1B 24
Meyrick Rd. BH1—4D 24
Michelgrove Rd. BH5—4H 25
Michelmersh Grn. BH8—2G 13
Mickleham Clo. BH12—5G 11
Middle Rd. BH10—6H 5
Middle Rd. BH15—1F 21
Middleton Rd. BH9—2B 12
Midland Rd. BH9—4C 12
Midwood Av. BH8—4H 13
Milborne Cres. BH12—5D 10
Milburn Rd. BH4—3G 23
Milestone Rd. BH15—1E 21
Milford Dri. BH11—6E 5
Millfield. BH17—6C 8
Millhams Clo. BH10—5G 5
Millhams Dri. BH10—4G 5
Millhams Rd. BH10—4F 5
Millhams St. BH23—1H 27
Millhams St. N. BH23—6H 15
Mill Hill Clo. BH14—4A 22
Mill La. BH11—4A 22
Mill La. BH23—5D 18
Mill Rd. BH23—5G 15
Mill Rd. N. BH8—2G 13
Mill Rd. S. BH8—3F 13
Millstream Clo. BH17—5B 8
Mill St. BH21—1A 2
Milne Rd. BH17—4C 8
Milner Rd. BH4—5H 23
Milton Clo. BH25—3H 19
Milton Gro. BH25—3G 19
Milton Mead. BH23—3G 19
Milton Rd. BH8—2D 24
Milton Rd. BH14—4C 22
Milverton Clo. BH23—3A 18
Mimosa Av. BH21—2F 3
Minstead Rd. BH10—1H 11
Minterne Rd. BH9—3D 12
Minterne Rd. BH14—2B 30
Minterne Rd. BH23—1C 28
Mission La. BH18—2B 8
Mission Rd. BH18—2B 8
Mitchell Clo. BH25—6H 19
Mitchell Rd. BH17—5G 9
Moat La. BH25—4G 19
Moffat Rd. BH23—6B 16
Monks Way. BH11—6C 4
Monksmill Grn. BH23—1B 28
Monkton Cres. BH12—5E 11
Montacute Way. BH21—3F 3
Montague Rd. BH5—3B 26
Montagu Pk. BH25—5C 18
Montagu Rd. BH23—5C 18
Montgomery Av. BH11—1C 12
Montrose Dri. BH10—3G 11
Moonrakers Way. BH23—4H 17
Moorcroft Av. BH23—2A 16
Moordown Clo. BH9—1C 12
Moore Av. BH11—6F 5 to 2F 11
Moore Clo. BH25—6G 19
Moorfield Gro. BH9—3C 12
Moorfields Rd. BH13—1E 31
Moorings, The. BH3—5A 12
Moorings, The. BH23—2G 27
Moorland Av. BH25—4G 19

Moorland Rd. BH1—3F 25
Moor Rd. BH18—6C 2
Moorside Clo. BH11—1G 11
Moorside Rd. BH11—2F 11
Moortown Dri. BH21—2A 4
Moorvale Rd. BH9—3D 12
Moor View Rd. BH15—6G 9
Morden Rd. BH9—3B 12
Moreton Rd. BH9—1E 13
Morley Clo. BH23—1A 16
Morley Rd. BH5—2B 26
Mornish Rd. BH13—5E 23
Morrison Av. BH12—6E 11
Mortimer Clo. BH23—1E 29
Mortimer Rd. BH8—4E 13
Mossley Av. BH12—4E 11
Motcombe Rd. BH13—5F 23
Mount Av. BH25—3H 19
Mountbatten Clo. BH23—1D 28
Mountbatten Gdns. BH8—3A 14
Mountbatten Rd. BH13 & BH4
　　　　　　　—6G 23
Mount Clo. BH25—4H 19
Mt. Grace Dri. BH14—2C 30
Mountjoy Clo. BH21—3H 1
Mt. Pleasant Dri. BH8—4H 13
Mt. Pleasant Rd. BH15—4F 21
Mount Rd. BH11—1F 11
Mount Rd. BH14—2A 22
Mt. Stuart Rd. BH5—4G 25
Mudeford. BH23
　　　　　—2C 28 to 2E 29
Mudeford Grn. Clo. BH23
　　　　　　　—2D 28
Mudeford La. BH23—1C 27
(in two parts)
Mude Gdns. BH23—2E 29
Mullins Clo. BH12—5H 11
Munster Rd. BH14—4C 22
Murley Rd. BH9—5D 12
Muscliffe La. BH9—1C 12
Muscliffe Rd. BH9—4C 12
Myrtle Rd. BH8—1F 25

Nada Rd. BH23—4G 17
Nairn Rd. BH3—1B 24
Nairn Rd. BH3—2D 30
Naish Holiday Village. BH25
　　　　　　　—6D 18
Naish Rd. BH25—5F 19
Namu Rd. BH9—4A 12
Nansen Av. BH15—2F 21
Naseby Rd. BH9—3D 12
Nea Clo. BH23—5H 17
Nea Rd. BH23—5H 17
Nelson Clo. BH25—2G 19
Nelson Dri. BH23—1D 28
Nelson Rd. BH12 & BH4—3F 23
Netherhall Gdns. BH4—4H 23
Netley Clo. BH15—6H 9
Newbury Dri. BH10—3A 12
Newcombe Rd. BH6—1E 27
Newcroft Gdns. BH23—5G 15
Newfoundland Dri. BH15 & BH14
　　　　　　　—5E 21
New Harbour Rd. BH15
New Harbour Rd. S. BH15
　　　　　　　—6C 20
New Harbour Rd. W. BH15
　　　　　　　—6C 20
Newlands Rd. BH7—1A 26
Newlands Rd. BH23—6D 16
Newlands Way. BH18—2A 8
Newlyn Way. BH12—6D 10
Newmorton Rd. BH9—6C 6
New Orchard. BH15—5D 20
New Pde. BH10—2B 12
New Pk. Rd. BH6—2C 26
New Quay Rd. BH15—6C 20
New Rd. BH10—5B 6
New Rd. BH12—1C 12

New Rd. BH22 BH10
　　　　　—1B to 5B 6
Newstead Rd. BH6—3D 26
New St. BH15—6D 20
Newton Rd. BH13—1E 31
Nicholas Clo. BH23—3C 18
Nicholas Gdns. BH10—3H 11
Nicholson Clo. BH17—5G 9
Nightingale La. BH15—5D 20
Nightjar Clo. BH17—5A 8
Noble Clo. BH11—3E 11
Noel Rd. BH10—3G 11
Norcliffe Clo. BH11—2G 11
Norfolk Av. BH23—3F 15
Norleywood. BH23—5A 18
Norman Av. BH12—1F 23
Normandy Dri. BH23—6B 16
Normandy Gdns. BH12—1F 23
Normanhurst Av. BH8—4G 13
Normanton Clo. BH23—4F 15
Norris Gdns. BH25—3H 19
Norrish Rd. BH12—2E 23
North Av. BH10—4A 6
Northbourne Av. BH10—6A 6
Northbourne Gdns. BH10—6A 6
Northbourne Pl. BH10—6A 6
Northbrook Rd. BH18—3B 8
Northcote Rd. BH1—3E 25
Northey Rd. BH6—1E 27
N. Lodge Rd. BH14—3D 22
Northmead Dri. BH17—5B 8
Normere Dri. BH12—6E 11
Northmere Rd. BH12—6E 11
Northover. BH3—1B 24
North Rd. BH7—2H 25
North Rd. BH14—3G 21
North St. BH15—5E 21
N. Wood. BH25—5E 19
Nortoft Rd. BH8—1D 24
Norton Clo. BH23—6B 16
Norton Rd. BH9—4A 12
Norwich Av. BH2—4A 24
Norwich Av. W. BH2—4A 24
Norwich Rd. BH2—4B 24
Norwood Pl. BH5—2B 26
Noyce Gdns. BH8—3B 14
Nuffield Rd. BH17—6E 9
Nugent Rd. BH6—2C 26
Nursery Rd. BH9—2D 12
Nursling Grn. BH8—6G 13
Nuthatch Clo. BH17—5B 8
Nutley Clo. BH11—1E 11
Nutley Way. BH11—1E 11

Oak Av. BH23—5E 15
Oak Clo. BH22—2A 6
Oakdale Rd. BH15—1F 21
Oakfield Rd. BH15—1E 21
Oakford Ct. BH8—2F 13
Oakland Wlk. BH22—1B 6
Oakleigh Way. BH23—6A 18
Oakley Clo. BH23—1F 3
Oakley La. BH21—1F 3
Oakley Rd. BH21—1F 3
Oakley Straight. BH21—1F 3
Oakmead Rd. BH17—5B 8
Oak Rd. BH8—1F 25
Oakwood. BH3—6B 12
Oakwood Clo. BH9—3D 12
Oakwood Rd. BH9—3D 12
Oakwood Rd. BH23—4A 18
Oates Rd. BH9—3B 12
Oban Rd. BH3—6B 12
Okeford Rd. BH18—2D 8
Old Barn Clo. BH23—2D 14
Old Barn Rd. BH23—3D 14
Old Bridge Rd. BH6—5D 26
Old Christchurch La. BH1
　　　　　　　—4C 24
Old Christchurch Rd. BH1
　　　　　　　—4C 24
Old Coastguard Rd. BH13
　　　　　　　—6A 30

Old Farm Rd. BH15—6F 9
Old Grn. Pde. BH25—4G 19
Old Milton Grn. BH25—4G 19
Old Milton Rd. BH25—4H 19
Old Orchard. BH15—6D 20
Old Priory Rd. BH14—3F 27
Old Rope Wlk. BH15—6B 20
Old Vicarage Clo. BH10—5B 6
Old Wareham Rd. BH17
　　　　　—6D 8 to 5A 10
Ophir Gdns. BH8—2E 25
Ophir Rd. BH8—2D 24
Oratory Gdns. BH13—1E 31
Orchard Av. BH14—5G 21
Orchard Clo. BH23—5A 18
Orchard Gro. BH25—4H 19
Orchard St. BH2—4B 24
Orchestan Rd. BH8—1E 25
Orchid Way. BH23—6A 16
Orford Clo. BH23—1D 14
Ormonde Rd. BH13—5F 23
Osborne Rd. BH9—5B 12
Osborne Rd. BH14—4B 22
Osborne Rd. BH25—2H 19
Oswald Clo. BH9—3B 12
Oswald Rd. BH9—3B 12
Otter Rd. BH15—1H 21
Overbury Rd. BH14—4B 22
Overcombe Clo. BH17—2F 9
Over Links Dri. BH14—5C 22
Ovington Av. BH7—5C 14
Ovington Gdns. BH7—6D 14
Owls Rd. BH5—3G 25
Oxey Clo. BH25—4H 19
Oxford Av. BH6—2C 26
Oxford La. BH11—5G 5
Oxford Rd. BH8—3D 24

Paddington Gro. BH11—1C 10
Paddock. BH21—5D 18
Padfield Clo. BH6—1E 27
Paget Rd. BH11—1F 11
Paisley Rd. BH6—1C 26
Palfrey Rd. BH10—6A 6
Palma Apartments. BH25
　　　　　　　—5D 18
Palmer Rd. BH15—2D 20
Palmerston Av. BH23—1B 28
Palmerston Rd. BH1—2G 25
Palmerston Rd. BH14—3C 22
Panorama Rd. BH13—6A 30
Parade, The. BH6—4E 27
Paradise St. BH15—6D 20
Parham Rd. BH25—2G 19
Parham Rd. BH10—3H 11
Parish Rd. BH15—4F 21
Park Av. BH10—4H 5
Park Clo. BH23—2A 16
Parker Rd. BH9—5C 12
Park Gdns. BH23—6C 16
Parkland Dri. BH25—4G 19
Park La. BH10—1C 12
Park La. BH23—1F 3
Park Rd. BH8—2D 24
Park Rd. BH14—3H 21
Park Rd. BH25—4G 19
Parkside. BH21—4H 17
Parkside Gdns. BH10—2B 12
Parkside Rd. BH14—3B 22
Parkstone Av. BH14—3C 22
Parkstone Heights. BH14
(in two parts)—1H 21
Parkstone Rd. BH15—4F 21
Park, The. BH25—5D 18
Parkway Dri. BH8—4G 13
Parkwood Rd. BH5—2A 26
Parley Clo. BH22—2B 6
Parley La. BH23—3D 6 to 4H 7
Parley Rd. BH9—2D 12
Parr St. BH14—3A 22
Parsonage Rd. BH1—4C 24
Partridge Dri. BH14—6B 22
Partridge Wlk. BH14—6B 22

Pascoe Clo. BH14—3A 22
Pasuntley Rd. BH23—1C 28
Pauncefote Rd. BH5—2A 26
Pavan Gdns. BH10—2H 11
Pearce Av. BH14—6H 21
Pearl Gdns. BH10—2H 11
Pearl Rd. BH10—1H 11
Pearson Av. BH14—2B 22
Pearson Gdns. BH10—5A 6
Peckham Av. BH25—2H 19
Peel Clo. BH12—2B 22
Pelham Clo. BH23—1B 28
Pembroke Rd. BH4—5G 23
Pembroke Rd. BH12—6C 10
Pengelly Av. BH10—6B 6
Pennant Way. BH23—6D 16
Penn Clo. BH25—4G 19
Penn Hill Av. BH14—4C 22
Penny Hedge. BH25—5H 19
Penrith Rd. BH5—3A 26
Percy Rd. BH5—3H 25
Peregrine Rd. BH23—1E 29
Pergin Cres. BH17—6C 8
Pergin Way. BH17—6C 8
Perryfield Gdns. BH7—5B 14
Perry Gdns. BH15—6E 21
Persley Rd. BH10—6A 6
Perth Clo. BH23—4E 15
Petersfield Pl. BH7—6B 14
Petersfield Rd. BH7—1B 26
Petersham Rd. BH17—5B 8
Petit Rd. BH9—1D 12
Phelipps Rd. BH21—4A 2
Phyldon Clo. BH12—1B 22
Phyldon Rd. BH12—1B 22
Pickering Clo. BH18—2C 8
Pickford Rd. BH9—4B 12
Pier App. BH1—5C 24
Pilgrims Way. BH17—5C 8
Pilot Hight Rd. BH11—1F 11
Pilsdon Dri. BH17—2G 9
Pimpern Clo. BH17—3G 9
Pine Av. BH6—3C 26
Pine Av. BH12—6E 11
Pine Av. BH21—1A 2
Pinesprings Dri. BH18—2A 8
Pine Tree Glen. BH4—4H 23
Pine Tree Wlk. BH17—5B 8
Pine Vale Cres. BH10—2B 12
Pinewood Av. BH10—6A 6
Pinewood Clo. BH10—5A 6
Pinewood Clo. BH23—3B 18
Pinewood Rd. BH13—6A 23
Pinewood Rd. BH25—3A 18
Pipers Dri. BH23—6E 17
Pippin Clo. BH23—3E 15
Pittmore Rd. BH23—2A 16
Pitwines Clo. BH15—6B 20
Plantagenet Cres. BH11—6C 4
Plantation Dri. BH23—3B 18
Plantation Rd. BH17—4H 17
Plassey Cres. BH11—6C 4
Playfields Dri. BH12—1D 22
Pleasance Way. BH25—2G 19
Plemont Clo. BH12—4D 10
Plumer Rd. BH17—4C 8
Ponsonby Rd. BH14—2H 23
Poole Hill. BH2—4A 24
Poole La. BH11—1D 10 to 5G 5
Poole Rd. BH4 & BH2—3G 23
Poole Rd. BH12—3E 23
Popes Rd. BH15—1F 21
Poplar Clo. BH25—5C 18
Poppy Clo. BH23—4F 15
Portarlington Clo. BH4—5A 24
Portarlington Rd. BH4—4H 23

Portchester Pl. BH8—2E 25
Portchester Rd. BH8—1D 24
Portelet Clo. BH23—3C 10
Porter Rd. BH17—5C 8
Portesham Gdns. BH9—1E 13
Portesham Way. BH17—2F 9
Portfield Clo. BH23—5G 15
Portfield Rd. BH23—5F 15
Portland Rd. BH9—4C 12
Portman Cres. BH5—3C 26
Portman Rd. BH7—2H 25
Portswood Dri. BH10—1C 14
Post Office Rd. BH1—4C 24
Potters Way. BH14—5B 22
Pottery Rd. BH14—4A 22
Pound Clo. BH15—1G 21
Pound La. BH15—2F 21
Pound La. BH23—1H 27
Powell Rd. BH14—4A 22
Powerscourt Rd. BH25—6F 19
Preston La. BH23—2B 16
Preston Rd. BH15—1D 20
Preston Way. BH23—5G 17
Prestwood Clo. BH25—6G 19
Priestley Rd. BH10—4G 11
Primrose Gdns. BH17—4B 8
Primrose Way. BH21—4A 2
Primrose Way. BH23—4F 17
Prince of Wales Rd. BH4—3G 23
Princess Av. BH23—1H 27
Princess Rd. BH4 & BH12
(in two parts)—3F & 3G 23
Priors Clo. BH23—6G 17
Priors Rd. BH17—6G 17
Priory Ind. Pk. BH9—6F 17
Priory Rd. BH2—5B 24
Priory View Pl. BH9—1D 12
Priory View Rd. BH9—2D 12
Priory View Rd. BH23—2A 16
Privet Rd. BH9—4B 12
Promenade. BH13—4D 30
(Canford Cliffs)
Promenade. BH13—5C 30
(Sandbanks)
Promenade. BH15—6A 20
(Lower Hamworthy)
Promenade. BH15—3D 20
(Sterte)
Promenade. BH23—2F 29
(in two parts)
Prosperous St. BH15—5D 20
Puddletown Cres. BH17—3G 9
Purbeck Av. BH15—6A 20
Purbeck Rd. BH2—4B 24
Purbeck Rd. BH25—6E 19
Purewell. BH23—1A 28
Purewell Cross Rd. BH23
　　　　　　　—6A 16
Purewell M. BH23—6B 16
Pye Clo. BH21—4A 2

Quayle Dri. BH11—5E 5
Quay Rd. BH23—1H 27
Quay, The. BH15—6D 20
Quay, The. BH23—2A 28
Queen Anne Dri. BH23—3E 3
Queen Mary Av. BH9—3C 12
Queens Av. BH23—1H 27
Queen's Gdns. BH2—3A 24
Queensland Rd. BH5—2A 26
Queen's Pk. Av. BH8—5E 13
Queens Pk. Gdns. BH8—6E 13
Queens Pk. Rd. BH8—6E 13
Queens Pk. S. Dri. BH8—6F 13
Queens Pk. W. Dri. BH8—6F 13
Queen's Rd. BH2—4A 24
Queens Rd. BH14—3C 22
Queen's Rd. BH23—1C 28
Queensway. BH23—2B 16
Queenswood Av. BH8—4H 13
Quintin Clo. BH23—5A 18

Radipole Rd. BH17—3H 9
Railway Ter. BH23—3A 18
Raleigh Clo. BH23—2D 28
Raleigh Clo. BH25—2G 19
Raleigh Rd. BH12—3D 10
Ralph Rd. BH21—4A 2
Randolph Rd. BH1—3G 25
Randolph Rd. BH14—2B 22
Ranelagh Rd. BH23—6A 18
Ravenscourt Rd. BH6—2C 26
Ravensdale Clo. BH12—1B 22
Raven Way. BH23—2E 29
Ravine Rd. BH5—3B 26
Ravine Rd. BH13—1E 31
Rebbeck Rd. BH7—1A 26
Recreation Rd. BH12—1D 22
Rectory Rd. BH15—1D 20
Redan Clo. BH23—6B 18
Redbreast Rd. BH9—2D 12
Redbreast Rd. N. BH9—1D 12
Redcliffe Clo. BH23—2A 16
Redhill Av. BH9—3B 12
Redhill Clo. BH10—2B 12
Redhill Cres. BH9—2C 12
Redhill Rd. BH10—3B 12
Redhoave Rd. BH17—3F 9
Redlands. BH12—2E 23
Redshank Clo. BH17—4B 8
Redvers Rd. BH23—5C 16
Regent Dri. BH7—5A 14
Regent Way. BH23—1H 27
Reid St. BH23—5G 15
Rempstone Rd. BH21—2F 3
Renault Dri. BH18—4B 8
Ribble Clo. BH18—2C 8
Ricardo Cres. BH23—1E 29
Richmond Gdns. BH1—3C 24
Richmond Hill. BH2—4C 24
Richmond Pk. Av. BH8—6E 13
Richmond Pk. Clo. BH8—6E 13
Richmond Pk. Cres. BH8—6F 13
Richmond Pk. Dri. BH8—1F 25
Richmond Pk. Rd. BH8—6E 13
Richmond Rd. BH14—2C 22
Richmond Wood Rd. BH8
　　　　　　　—6E 13
Ridgefield Gdns. BH23—5H 17
Ridgemount Gdns. BH15—4A 20
Ridgeway. BH18—1C 8
Ridge Way. BH22—2B 6
Ridley Rd. BH5—5C 12
Riggs Gdns. BH11—3E 11
Rigler Rd. BH15—6B 20
Ringwood Rd. BH11 & BH22
　　　　　—2D 10 to 1G 5
Ringwood Rd. BH14 & BH12
　　　　—3G 21 to 5A 10
Ringwood Rd. BH23
　　　　　—1H 17 to 4D 18
Ringwood Rd. S. BH12—5A 10
Ripon Rd. BH9—5C 12
Ritchie Rd. BH11—1G 11
Riverdale La. BH23—1G 27
Riverlea Rd. BH23—1G 27
Rivermead Gdns. BH23—3E 15
Riversdale Rd. BH6—3G 27
Riverside. BH10—6C 6
Riverside Av. BH7—5C 14
Riverside La. BH6—4F 27
Riverside Rd. BH23—2G 27
Riverside Rd. BH6—3G 27
River Way. BH23—3D 14
R. L. Stevenson Av. BH4—4G 23
Roberts La. BH17—5B 8
Roberts Rd. BH7—1B 26
Roberts Rd. BH17—4C 8
Robins Way. BH23—2F 29
Robsall Clo. BH12—6D 10
Rochester Rd. BH11—1G 11
Rockford Clo. BH6—2F 27
Rockley Rd. BH15—5A 20
Rodney Clo. BH23—5F 11

Rodney Dri. BH23—1D 28
Rodwell Clo. BH10—5H 5
Roeshot Cres. BH23—4H 17
Roeshot Hill. BH23—3F 17
Rolls Dri. BH6—3H 27
Roman Heights. BH21—3A 2
Roman Rd. BH17, BH18 & BH21
—5A 8 to 4A 2
Romney Clo. BH10—1B 12
Romney Rd. BH10—1B 12
Rook Hill Rd. BH23—1F 29
Roosevelt Cres. BH11—5G 5
Ropley Rd. BH7—6C 14
Rosamund Av. BH21—2F 3
Roscrea Clo. BH6—3H 27
Roscrea Dri. BH6—3H 27
Roseberry Rd. BH5—2B 26
Rosebud Av. BH9—2C 12
Rose Cres. BH15—6G 9
Rosedale Clo. BH23—6C 16
Rose Gdns. BH9—2C 12
Rosemary Rd. BH12—5A 10
Rosemount Rd. BH4—5G 23
Rosewood Gdns. BH6—1G 19
Roslin La. BH3—6B 12
Roslin Rd. S. BH3—6A 12
Ross Gdns. BH11—6C 4
Ross Glades. BH3—1B 24
Rossley Clo. BH23—3A 18
Rossmore Rd. BH12—5B 10
Rotherfield Rd. BH5—3B 26
Rotherfield Rd. BH23—4B 18
Rothersay Dri. BH23—6A 18
Rothesay Rd. BH4—1H 23
Rotterdam Dri. BH23—6B 16
Roumelia La. BH5—3G 25
Roundhayle Rd. BH11—5E 5
Roundways. BH11—2E 11
Rowan Clo. BH23—5H 17
Rowan Dri. BH17—4A 8
Rowan Dri. BH23—5G 17
Rowbarrow Clo. BH17—3G 9
Rowena Rd. BH6—2F 27
Rowland Av. BH11—1F 21
Rownhams Rd. BH8—2F 13
Royal Arc. BH1—3H 25
Royal Oak Rd. BH10—5H 5
Rozelle Rd. BH14—3B 22
Rubens Clo. BH25—1H 19
Rufford Gdns. BH6—2E 27
Rugby Rd. BH17—4C 8
Runnymede Av. BH11—4C 4
Runton Rd. BH12—2E 23
Runway, The. BH23—6F 17
Rushcombe Way. BH21—5A 2
Rushford Warren. BH23—2D 28
Rushmere Rd. BH6—6D 14
Rushton Cres. BH23—1C 24
Ruskin Av. BH9—1D 12
Russell Cotes Rd. BH1—5D 24
Russell Rd. BH23—1B 28
Russel Rd. BH10—5H 5
Rutland Rd. BH9—5D 12
Rutland Rd. BH23—4F 15
Ryall Dri. BH17—4E 9
Ryan Gdns. BH11—5G 5
Rydal Clo. BH23—1E 14
Ryecroft Av. BH11—6E 5

Saffron Dri. BH23—5F 17
St Albans Av. BH8—6E 13
St Albans Cres. BH8—5E 13
St Albans Rd. BH8—6E 13
St Aldhelm's Rd. BH13—4E 23
St Andrew's Rd. BH18—5C 2
St Anne's Av. BH6—2E 27
St Anthony's Rd. BH2—2B 24
St Aubyn's Ct. BH15—5D 20
St Augustin's Rd. BH2—1C 24
St Brelade's Av. BH12—3C 10
St Catherine's Hill La. BH23
—3F 15

St Catherine's Pde. BH23
—3F 15
St Catherine's Path. BH6
—4E 27
St Catherine's Rd. BH6—3F 27
St Catherine's Way. BH23
—2D 14
St Clair Rd. BH13—3E 31
St Clement's Gdns. BH1—2G 25
St Clement's Rd. BH1—2F 25
St Clement's Rd. BH15—6A 10
St Denys. BH25—3H 19
St George's Av. BH8—5F 13
St George's Av. BH12—5A 10
St George's Clo. BH23—5H 17
St Helier Rd. BH12—3C 10
St Ives Gdns. BH2—2C 24
St James's Clo. BH15—6D 20
St James's Sq. BH5—2A 26
St John's Rd. BH5—3G 25
St John's Rd. BH15—3F 21
St John's Rd. BH23—6D 16
St Ledger's Pl. BH8—1G 25
St Ledger's Rd. BH8—6G 13
St Leonard's Rd. BH8—1E 25
St Luke's Rd. BH9—6C 12
St Margaret's Av. BH23—1H 27
St Margaret's Rd. BH10—3G 11
St Margaret's Rd. BH15—3E 21
St Mark's Rd. BH11—2G 11
St Mary's Rd. BH1—1G 25
St Mary's Rd. BH15—4F 21
St Merrins Clo. BH10—1H 11
St Michael's Rd. BH2—4B 24
St Osmund's Rd. BH14—3C 22
St Paul's La. BH8—3D 24
(in two parts)
St Paul's Rd. BH8—3D 24
(in three parts)
St Peter's Rd. BH1—4C 24
St Peter's Rd. BH14—3H 21
St Stephen's Rd. BH2—3B 24
St Stephen's Way. BH2—3B 24
St Swithun's Rd. BH1—3E 25
St Swithun's Rd. S. BH1—4E 25
St Thomas Clo. BH10—2A 12
St Valerie Rd. BH2—2B 24
St Winifred's Rd. BH2—2C 24
Salisbury Rd. BH1—3G 25
Salisbury Rd. BH14—2B 22
Salisbury Rd. BH23
—1A to 5C 16
Salterns Rd. BH14—4A 22
Salterns Way. BH14—1A 30
Salter Rd. BH13—6B 30
Samples Way. BH17—5G 9
Samson Rd. BH15—4A 20
Sancreed Rd. BH12—6D 10
Sandbanks Rd. BH14
—4G 21 to 2C 30
Sandbourne Rd. BH4—6H 23
Sandbourne Rd. BH15—3F 21
Sandercotes Rd. BH14—3B 22
Sandford Clo. BH9—1F 13
Sandford Way. BH18—2B 8
Sandhills Clo. BH17—3F 9
Sandown Rd. BH23—6C 16
Sandpiper Clo. BH17—4B 8
Sandpit La. BH15—4F 21
Sandringham Clo. BH9—6E 7
Sandringham Gdns. BH9—6E 7
Sandringham Rd. BH14—3B 22
Sandyhurst Clo. BH17—4E 9
Sandy La. BH6—2C 26
Sandy La. BH22—1G 5
Sandy La. BH23—3E 15
Sandy Mead Rd. BH8—4H 13
Sandy Plot. BH23—4A 16
Sandy Way. BH10—1B 12
San Remo Towers. BH5—4H 25
Sarah Clo. BH7—5B 14
Sarf Rd. BH17—5G 9
Sark Rd. BH12—5C 10
Sarum Rd. BH15—6D 20

Saulfland Dri. BH23—5G 17
Saulfland Pl. BH23—5G 17
Saxonbury Rd. BH6—1F 27
Saxonford Rd. BH23—6G 17
Saxonhurst Clo. BH10—6B 6
Saxonhurst Rd. BH10—1A 12
Saxon Sq. BH23—1H 27
School La. BH11—5G 5
Scott Clo. BH12—4E 11
Scotter Rd. BH7—1B 26
Scott Rd. BH10—4E 11
Scott's Grn. BH23—5D 16
Scotts Hills La. BH23—6B 16
Seabourne Pl. BH5—2B 26
Seabourne Rd. BH5—2B 26
Seacombe Rd. BH13—6A 30
Seacroft Av. BH25—5F 19
Seafield Clo. BH25—6G 19
Seafield Dri. BH6—1E 27
Seafield Rd. BH6—3E 27
Seafield Rd. BH25—6F 17
Seafield Rd. BH25—6G 19
Seagull Rd. BH8—4F 13
Seamoor La. BH4—3G 23
Seamoor Rd. BH4—3G 23
Sea Rd. BH5—4G 25
Sea Rd. BH6—4F 27
Sea Rd. BH25—4F 19
Seaton Clo. BH23—5C 18
Seaton Rd. BH23—5C 18
Seatown Clo. BH17—3H 9
Sea View Rd. BH12—1A 22
Sea View Rd. BH23—3D 18
Sea View Rd. BH25—5E 19
Sea Vixen Ind. Est. BH23—6E 17
Seaward Av. BH6—3C 26
Seaward Av. BH25—6F 19
Seaward Path. BH13—1F 31
Seaway Av. BH23—6G 17
Second Marine Av. BH25
—6H 19
Sedgley Rd. BH9—5B 12
Selby Clo. BH18—1C 8
Seldown Bridge. BH15—5E 21
Seldown La. BH15—4A 21
Seldown Rd. BH15—4F 21
Selfridge Av. BH6—4H 27
Selfridge Clo. BH6—4H 27
Seliot Clo. BH15—2F 21
Selkirk Clo. BH21—2G 3
Selwood Caravan Pk. BH10
—4H 5
Selworthy Clo. BH14—5A 22
Serpentine La. N. BH15—4E 21
Serpentine Rd. BH15—4E 21
(in two parts)
Setley Gdns. BH8—2G 13
Sevenoaks Dri. BH7—5B 14
Shaftesbury Rd. BH8—1G 25
Shaftesbury Rd. BH15—3E 21
Shakespeare Rd. BH6—6D 14
Shapland Av. BH11—6D 4
Shapwick Rd. BH15—6C 20
Sharlands Clo. BH18—2D 8
Sharp Rd. BH12—6F 11
Shawford Gdns. BH8—2G 13
Shawford Rd. BH8—2G 13
Shelbourne Clo. BH8—1F 25
Shelbourne Rd. BH8—6D 12
Sheldrake Rd. BH23—2E 29
Shelley Clo. BH23—6G 17
Shelley Hill. BH23—6G 17
Shelley Rd. BH1 & BH7—2G 25
Shelley Rd. BH12—2C 22
Shelton Rd. BH6—1D 26
Shepherd Clo. BH23—4A 18
Shepherds Way. BH7—5B 14
Sherborn Cres. BH17—3G 9
Sherfield Clo. BH8—3F 13
Sheringham Rd. BH12—1E 23
Sherrin Clo. BH15—2E 21
Sherwood Av. BH14—5H 21
Sherwood Clo. BH23—5G 15
Shillingstone Dri. BH9—6E 7

Shillito Rd. BH12—2D 22
Shirley Rd. BH9—4D 12
Shirley Rd. BH12—1B 22
Shore Rd. BH13—3C 30
Short Clo. BH12—4F 11
Shorts Clo. BH23—4A 16
Shottsford Rd. BH15—1E 21
Sidney Gdns. BH9—6E 7
Silchester Clo. BH2—2C 24
Silverdale Clo. BH18—1A 8
Silver St. BH23—1H 27
Silver Way. BH23—5A 18
Silverwood Clo. BH21—1F 3
Simmonds Clo. BH15—2E 21
Singleton Dri. BH10—3H 11
Skinner St. BH15—6E 21
Skipton Clo. BH18—3B 8
Slades Farm Rd. BH10—3H 11
Slade's La. BH10—4H 11
Slepe Cres. BH12—5E 11
Slinn Rd. BH23—6C 16
Slip Way. BH15—5D 20
Smithfield Pl. BH9—4C 12
Smithson Clo. BH12—5G 11
Smugglers La. N. BH23
—5G to 3H 17
Smugglers La. S. BH23—5F 17
Smugglers View. BH25—6E 19
Smugglers Wood Rd. BH23
—4G 17
Snowdon Rd. BH4—3H 23
Snowdrop Gdns. BH23—4F 17
Soberton Rd. BH8—6G 13
Solent Dri. BH25—6H 19
Solent Rd. BH6—4G 27
Solent Rd. BH23—3D 18
Solent Rd. BH25—5E 19
Solly Clo. BH12—5D 10
Somerby Rd. BH15—1F 21
Somerford Av. BH23—5E 17
Somerford Rd. BH23—6C 16
Somerford Way. BH23—6C 16
Somerley Rd. BH9—5D 12
Somerset Rd. BH7—2A 26
Somerset Rd. BH23—5E 15
Somerville Rd. BH4—4A 24
Sonning Way. BH8—3E 13
Sopers La. BH17—4B 8
Soper's La. BH23—1G 27
Sopwith Clo. BH23—1F 29
Sopwith Cres. BH21—1F 3
Sorrell Gdns. BH18—2B 8
Sorrell Way. BH23—5F 17
Southbourne Cliff Dri. BH6
—4F 27
Southbourne Coast Rd. BH6
—4E 27
Southbourne Gro. BH6—3C 26
Southbourne Overcliffe Dr BH6
—4C 26
Southbourne Prom. BH6—4C 26
Southbourne Rd. BH6
—1B to 3D 26
Southbrook Clo. BH17—3H 9
Southcliffe Rd. BH23—6F 17
Southcliffe Rd. BH25—5E 19
S. Cliff Rd. BH2—5C 24
Southcote Rd. BH1—3E 25
Southern La. BH25—5G 19
Southern Oaks. BH25—4G 19
Southern Rd. BH6—3C 26
Southey Rd. BH23—5D 16
Southill Av. BH12—6C 10
Southill Gdns. BH9—4D 12
Southill Rd. BH9—4D 12
Southill Rd. BH12—1C 22
S. Kinson Dri. BH11—1F 11
Southlands Av. BH6—3F 27
Southlands Av. BH21—5A 2
Southlea Av. BH6—2F 27
South Pk. Rd. BH12—5F 11
South Rd. BH1—2G 25
South Rd. BH15—5E 21
South Rd. BH21—4A 2
Stirling Clo. BH3—5B 12

S. View Pl. BH2—4B 24
S. View Rd. BH23—1G 27
Southville Rd. BH5—2B 26
S. Western Cres. BH14—5A 22
Southwick Pl. BH6—6D 14
Southwick Rd. BH6—1C 26
Southwood Av. BH6—3C 26
Southwood Av. BH23—4C 18
Southwood Clo. BH23—3C 18
Sovereign Centre. BH1—2H 25
Sovereign Clo. BH7—5A 14
Sparkford Clo. BH7—5B 14
Speedwell Dri. BH25—5F 17
Spencer Rd. BH1—3F 25
Spencer Rd. BH13—1D 30
Spencer Rd. BH25—2H 19
Spetisbury Clo. BH9—2E 13
Spicer La. BH11—6D 4
Springbank Rd. BH7—5A 14
Springdale Av. BH18—6B 2
Springdale Gro. BH21—1A 8
Springdale Rd. BH21 & BH18
—1A 8
Springfield Av. BH6—3G 27
Springfield Av. BH23—3D 14
Springfield Cres. BH14—3A 22
Springfield Rd. BH14—2A 22
Spring Gdns. BH12—2C 22
Spring Rd. BH7—1A 26
Springvale Av. BH7—5A 14
Springwater Clo. BH11—1F 11
Springwater Rd. BH11—1F 11
Spruce Clo. BH17—4A 8
Spurgeon Rd. BH7—1A 26
Spur Hill Av. BH14—4C 22
Spur Rd. BH14—4C 22
Square, The. BH2—4B 24
Squirrels Clo. BH23—3D 14
Stacey Clo. BH12—6C 10
Stacey Gdns. BH8—2H 13
Stafford Rd. BH1—4D 24
Stalbridge Rd. BH17—6C 8
Stalham Rd. BH12—1E 23
Stamford Rd. BH6—2D 26
Stanfield Cld BH12—6C 10
Stanfield Rd. BH9—5B 12
Stanfield Rd. BH12—6C 10
Stanley Green Cres. BH15
—2D 20
Stanley Grn. Rd. BH15—2D 20
Stanley Rd. BH1—2E 25
Stanley Rd. BH15—6C 20
Stanley Rd. BH23—5C 18
Stanpit. BH23—1B 28
Staple Clo. La. BH15—6E 9
Station App. BH18—6C 2
Station Rd. BH10—2H 11
Station Rd. BH14—3A 22
Station Rd. BH15—6C 20
Station Rd. BH23—2A 18
Station Rd. BH23—6G 15
(Christchurch)
Station Rd. BH25—2H 19
Stedman Rd. BH25—2C 26
Steepdene. BH14—4A 22
Steeple Clo. BH17—2F 9
Steepleton Rd. BH18—2E 9
Stem La. BH25—2F 19
Stenhurst Rd. BH15—1F 21
Stephen Langton Dri. BH11
—6D 4
Sterte Av. BH15—3D 20
Sterte Av. W. BH15—3D 20
Sterte Clo. BH15—3D 20
Sterte Rd. BH15—4E 21
Stevenson Cres. BH14—4D 22
Stevenson Rd. BH6—4C 27
Stewart Clo. BH8—2F 25
Stewart Rd. BH8—1D 24
Stillmore Rd. BH11—2C 10
Stinsford Clo. BH9—6E 7
Stinsford Rd. BH17—5E 9
Stirling Way. BH23—1E 29
Stoborough Dri. BH18—3B 8
Stockbridge Clo. BH17—3A 10
Stokes Av. BH15—3E 21
Stone Gdns. BH8—4C 14
Stoke Wood Rd. BH3—1C 24
Stony La. BH23—1A 16 to 1A 28
Stony La. S. BH23—1A 28
Story La. BH18—1C 8
Stourbank Rd. BH23—1G 27
Stourcliffe Av. BH6—3C 26
Stourcroft Dri. BH23—3E 15
Stourfield Rd. BH5—2B 26
Stourpaine Rd. BH17—3F 9
Stour Rd. BH8—1F 25
Stour Rd. BH23—2F 27 to 6G 15
Stourvale Av. BH23—5E 15
Stourvale Pl. BH5—2B 26
Stourvale Rd. BH5 & BH6
—2B 26
Stour View Gdns. BH21—2A 2
Stour Way. BH23—3D 14
Stourwood Av. BH6—4D 26
Stourwood Rd. BH6—3D 26
Strand St. BH15—6D 20
Stratfield Pl. BH25—2G 19
Strathmore Rd. BH9—6C 6
Stratton Rd. BH9—1E 13
Strete Mt. BH23—6C 16
Strouden Av. BH8—4E 13
Strouden Rd. BH9
—4C 12 to 4E 13
Stroud Gdns. BH23—1C 28
Stroud La. BH23—1C 28
Stroud Pk. Av. BH23—6C 16
Stuart Rd. BH23—5C 18
Studland Rd. BH4—6H 23
Studley Clo. BH23—5D 18
Sturminster Rd. BH9—1E 13
Suffolk Av. BH23—3F 15
Suffolk Rd. BH2
(in two parts)
Suffolk Rd. S. BH2—3A 24
Summerfield Clo. BH23—2A 16
Summerfields. BH17—2F 9
Summers Av. BH11—5G 5
Summer's La. BH23—4B 16
Sunbury Clo. BH11—5F 5
Sunderland Dri. BH23—6F 17
Sundew Rd. BH18—3A 8
Sunningdale Cres. BH10—1H 11
Sunnyfield Rd. BH25—5H 19
Sunnyhill Rd. BH6—2C 26
Sunny Hill Rd. BH12—2C 22
Sunnylands Av. BH6—3F 27
Sunnymoor Rd. BH11—4F 11
Sunnyside Rd. BH12—6C 10
Sunridge Clo. BH17—1F 23
Surrey Clo. BH23—3G 15
Surrey Gdns. BH4—3H 23
Surrey Rd. BH4—3H 23
Surrey Rd. BH12, BH4 & BH2
—2F 23
Surrey Rd. S. BH4—3H 23
Sussex Clo. BH9—6E 7
Sutherland Av. BH18—6A 2
Sutton Clo. BH17—3A 10
Sutton Rd. BH9—4D 12
Swallow Clo. BH15—5B 8
Swanmore Rd. BH7—1B 26
Swansbury Dri. BH8—3B 14
Sway Gdns. BH8—2G 13
Swift Clo. BH17—5B 8
Swordfish Dri. BH23—6E 17
Sycamore Clo. BH17—4A 8
Sycamore Rd. BH23—5E 15
Sydling Clo. BH17—3H 9
Sydney Rd. BH18—2E 9
Sydney Rd. BH23—4E 15
Sylmor Gdns. BH9—3D 12
Sylvan Rd. BH12—1B 22
Symes Rd. BH15—2A 20

Tadden Wlk. BH18—2B 8
Tait Clo. BH17—5G 9
Talbot Av. BH10, BH9 & BH3
—5A 12
Talbot Ct. BH9—4C 12
Talbot Dri. BH12—5G 11
Talbot Dri. BH23—3A 18
Talbot Hill Rd. BH9—5A 12
Talbot Meadows. BH12—5G 11
Talbot Rise. BH10—3H 11
Talbot Rd. BH9—5A 12
Tamworth Rd. BH7—2A 26
Tangmere Clo. BH23—6E 17
Tan Howse Clo. BH7—5B 14
Tarn Dri. BH17—4B 8
Tarrent Clo. BH17—2F 9
Tarrent Rd. BH9—2E 13
Tatnam La. BH15—3E 21
Tatnam Rd. BH15—3E 21
Taverner Clo. BH15—6F 21
Taylors Bldgs. BH15—6D 20
Tedder Clo. BH11—1G 11
Tedder Gdns. BH11—2G 11
Tedder Rd. BH11—2G 11
Templer Clo. BH11—3E 11
Tennyson Rd. BH9—2C 12
Tennyson Rd. BH14—4H 21
Tensing Rd. BH23—5C 16
Terence Av. BH11—3E 9
Terrace Rd. BH2—4B 24
Terrington Av. BH23—3H 17
Thames St. BH15—6D 20
Thetford Rd. BH12—1E 23
Third Marine Av. BH25—6H 19
Thistlebarrow Rd. BH7—6H 13
Thoresby Ct. BH25—2F 19
Thornbury Rd. BH6—3G 27
Thorncombe Clo. BH9—1E 13
Thorncombe Clo. BH17—3G 9
Thornfield Dri. BH23—4A 18
Thornley Rd. BH10—6A 6
Thorn Rd. BH17—2E 8
Three Acre Clo. BH25—4G 19
Three Acre Dri. BH25—4G 19
Throop Clo. BH8—3A 14
Throop Rd. BH8—6G 7 to 4B 14
(in two parts)
Throopside Av. BH9—1F 13
Thrush Rd. BH12—4A 10
Thursby Rd. BH23—3A 18
Thwaite Rd. BH12—2G 23
Tilburg Rd. BH23—6B 16
Timothy Clo. BH10—6A 6
Tincleton Gdns. BH9—1E 13
Todber Clo. BH11—1D 10
Tollard Clo. BH12—5D 10
Tollerford Rd. BH17—3F 9
Tolpuddle Gdns. BH9—1E 13
Tolstoi Rd. BH14—1H 21
Tonge Rd. BH11—5G 5
Torbay Rd. BH14—4B 22
Totmel Rd. BH17—3H 9
Tourney Rd. BH11—5D 4
Tower Pk. BH12—4A 10
Tower Rd. BH1—2G 25
Tower Rd. BH13—5G 23
Tower Rd. W. BH13—6F 23
Towers Farm. BH21—4A 2
Towngate Bri. BH15—5D 20
Townsend Clo. BH11—5G 5
Townsville Rd. BH9—2E 13
Tozer Clo. BH11—3E 11
Trafalgar Ct. BH23—1D 28
Trafalgar Rd. BH9—5C 12
Treebys Clo. BH23—3G 17
Treeside. BH23—3G 17
Tregonwell Rd. BH2—4B 24
Trentham Av. BH7—5B 14
Trentham Clo. BH7—5B 14
Tresillian Clo. BH23—3C 18
Tresillian Way. BH23—3C 18
Triangle, The. BH2—4B 24
Triangle, The. BH25—5G 18
Trigon Rd. BH15—6F 9
Trinidad Cres. BH12—5B 10

Trinity Rd. BH1—3D 24
Troon Rd. BH18—6C 2
Truman Rd. BH11—5G 5
Truscott Av. BH9—6C 12
Tuckers La. BH15—6B 20
Tuckton Clo. BH6—3D 26
Tuckton Rd. BH6—3D 26
Tudor Ct. BH15—1G 21
Tudor Rd. BH18—6C 2
Turbary Clo. BH12—5D 10
Turbary Heights. BH11—3E 11
Turbary Pk. Av. BH11—1E 11
Turbary Rd. BH12—5C 10
Turks La. BH14—6H 21
Turnworth Clo. BH18—1E 9
Tweedale Rd. BH9—1E 13
Twemlow Av. BH14—5G 21
Twin Oaks Clo. BH18—2C 8
Twyford Clo. BH8—3G 13
Twyford Way. BH17—3F 9
Twynham Av. BH23—6G 15
Twynham Rd. BH6—4E 27
Tyndale Cres. BH9—6E 7
Tyneham Av. BH12—5B 10
Tyrell Gdns. BH8—2A 14
Tytherley Grn. BH8—3G 13

Ullswater Rd. BH21—1E 3
Undercliff Dri. BH1 & BH5
—5C 24 to 4G 25
Undercliff Rd. BH5—4G 25
Underwood Clo. BH17—4D 8
Uplands Av. BH25—5H 19
Uplands Rd. BH8—3E 13
Up. Golf Links Rd. BH18—6D 2
Up. Gordon Rd. BH12—4A 10
Up. Hinton Rd. BH1—4C 24
Up. Norwich Rd. BH2—4A 24
Upper Rd. BH12—6B 10
Up. Terrace Rd. BH2—4B 24
Uppleby Rd. BH12—2B 22
Upton Rd. BH17—6A to 6D 8
(in two parts)
Upton Way. BH18—2A 8
Upwey Av. BH15—5D 20
Utrecht Ct. BH23—6B 16

Valencia Clo. BH23—1D 14
Vale Rd. BH1—3F 25
Vale Rd. BH14—2D 22
Valette Rd. BH9—1D 12
Valiant Way. BH23—6E 17
Valley Clo. BH23—2E 15
Valley Rd. BH8—2H 13
Valley View. BH12—5G 11
Vallis Clo. BH15—6E 21
Vanguard Rd. BH8—4H 13
Vanguard Rd. BH15—5E 21
Vecta Clo. BH23—2E 15
Vectis Rd. BH25—5E 19
Venning Av. BH11—6D 4
Verity Cres. BH17—4G 9
Vernalls Clo. BH10—5A 6
Vernalls Gdns. BH10—5A 6
Verney Clo. BH11—2G 11
Verona Av. BH6—2D 26
Verulam Pl. BH1—4C 24
Verulam Rd. BH14—3G 21
Verwood Cres. BH6—3H 27
Vetch Clo. BH23—5F 17
Vicarage Rd. BH9—3B 12
Vicarage Rd. BH15—1E 21
Vicarage Way. BH23—2B 16
Vickers Clo. BH8—3B 14
Victoria Av. BH9—3B 12
Victoria Cres. BH12—1C 22
Victoria Pl. BH1—2F 25
Victoria Rd. BH1—2F 25
Victoria Rd. BH12—2B 22
Victoria Rd. BH23—2C 28
Viking Clo. BH6—3G 27
Viking Way. BH6—3G 27
Viking Way. BH23—2E 29

Villette Clo. BH23—4G 15
Vince Clo. BH11—5G 5
Vincent Clo. BH25—2H 19
Vincent Rd. BH25—2H 19
Vine Clo. BH7—5B 14
Vine Farm Clo. BH12—5H 11
Vine Farm Rd. BH12—5G 11
Vinneys Clo. BH23—3A 16
Virginia Clo. BH12—6B 10
Viscount Dri. BH23—6E 17
Viscount Wlk. BH11—6C 4
Vulcan Way. BH23—6F 17

Wakefield Av. BH10—6A 6
Wakely Rd. BH11—5F 5
Walcott Av. BH23—4F 15
Walditch Gdns. BH17—3F 9
Waldren Clo. BH15—5F 21
Walkford La. BH25—3E 19
Walkford Rd. BH23—3D 18
Walkford Way. BH23—4C 18
Walkwood Av. BH7—5C 14
Wallace Rd. BH18—2C 8
Walliscott Rd. BH11—3F 11
Wallisdown Rd. BH12 & BH10
—3D 10 to 5A 12
Wallop Rd. BH10—4G 11
Walpole Rd. BH11—2G 15
Walsford Rd. BH4—2H 23
Walsingham Dene. BH7—5H 13
Waltham Rd. BH7—6B 14
Walton Clo. BH8—2A 14
Walton Rd. BH10—3H 11
Walton Rd. BH15—1H 21
Warburton Rd. BH17—4G 9
Wareham Rd. BH21—4A 2
Warland Way. BH21—4A 2
Warmwell Clo. BH9—1E 13
Warmwell Clo. BH17—3H 9
Warnford Rd. BH17 & BH6
—6B 14
Warren Av. BH23—2D 28
Warren Edge Clo. BH6—4F 27
Warren Edge Rd. BH6—4F 27
Warren Rd. BH4—5G 23
Warren Rd. BH14—3C 22
Warwick Pl. BH7—2A 26
Warwick Rd. BH7—2A 26
Warwick Rd. BH14—4B 22
Washington Av. BH1—1F 25
Watcombe Rd. BH6—2D 26
Waterditch Rd. BH23—2C 16
Waterford Rd. BH14—5A 22
Waterford Gdns. BH23—6B 18
Waterford Pl. BH23—5C 18
Waterford Rd. BH23—5C 18
Water La. BH6—5D 14
Waterloo Rd. BH9—6C 12
Waterloo Rd. BH17—6D 8
Watermead. BH23—2G 27
Watermill Rd. BH23—5C 18
Waterside. BH23—3D 28
Water Tower Rd. BH18—6D 2
Watery La. BH23—4E 17
Watkin Rd. BH5—3H 25
Wavell Av. BH17—4C 8
Wavell Rd. BH11—1G 11
Wavendon Av. BH25—5F 19
Waverley Cres. BH15—1F 21
Waverley Rd. BH1—3E 25
Waverley Rd. BH25—3H 19
Wayground Rd. BH21—1A 2
Wayman Rd. BH21—5A 2
Wayne Rd. BH12—1A 22
Wayside Rd. BH6—3E 27
Waytown Clo. BH17—4E 9
Webbs Way. BH11—3E 11
Webster Rd. BH9—2D 12
Wedgewood Dri. BH14—5A 22
Weldon Av. BH11—6D 4
Well Clo. BH25—3G 19
Wellesley Av. BH23—6F 17
Wellington Av. BH23—6G 17
Wellington Ct. BH25—1H 19
Wellington Rd. BH8—1C 24

Wellington Rd. BH14—4B 22
Well La. BH15—2E 21
Wendover Clo. BH25—6G 19
Wentworth Av. BH5—3B 26
Wentworth Clo. BH5—3B 26
Wentworth Dri. BH23—1F 27
Wescott Way. BH11—1D 10
Wesley Rd. BH12—2B 22
Wessex Av. BH25—3H 19
Wessex Clo. BH23—6F 17
Wessex Rd. BH14—4A 22
Wessex Trade Centre. BH15
—5A 10
Wessex Way. BH4, BH2, BH1 &
BH8—3G 23 to 4A 14
Westbourne Arc. BH4—4G 23
Westbourne Pk. Rd. BH4—5G 23
Westbury Clo. BH23—3G 17
Westbury Rd. BH25—4H 19
W. Butts St. BH15—5D 20
Westby Rd. BH5—3H 25
W. Cliff Gdns. BH2—5B 24
W. Cliff Prom. BH2—5B 24
W. Cliff Promenade. BH2
—5A 24
W. Cliff Rd. BH4 & BH2
—4G 23 to 5B 24
Westcroft Pde. BH25—3H 19
Westcroft Pk. BH18—1E 9
Westdown Rd. BH11—6F 5
Westerham Rd. BH4—4G 23
Western Av. BH10—6A 6
Western Av. BH13—4D 22
Western Av. BH25—4F 19
Western Clo. BH10—6A 6
Western Rd. BH13 & BH14
—1E 31 to 4G 23
Westfield Gdns. BH23—4F 17
Westfield Rd. BH6—3E 27
W. Ham Clo. BH9—4E 13
Westham Clo. BH17—1F 9
Westheath Rd. BH18—1C 8
W. Hill Pl. BH2—4A 24
W. Hill Rd. BH2—4A 24
W. Howe Clo. BH11—1F 9
West Howe Ind. Est. BH11
—2E 11
Westminster Ct. BH25—6G 19
Westminster Rd. BH13—6G 23
Westminster Rd. E. BH13
—6G 23
Weston Dri. BH1—4E 25
Westons La. BH15—5D 20
W. Overcliff Dri. BH4—5H 23
Westover Rd. BH1—4C 24
W. Quay Rd. BH15—6C 20
West Rd. BH5—2G 27
West St. BH15—6D 20
W. Undercliff Prom. BH2
—6A 24
W. View Rd. BH15—3D 20
Westview Rd. BH23—1C 28
West Way. BH9—2D 12
West Way. BH18—2B 8
Wetherby Clo. BH18—3C 8
Weyman's Av. BH10—4H 5
Weymans Dri. BH10—4H 5
Weymouth Rd. BH14—2B 22
Wharf Clo. BH12—1D 22
Wharfdale Rd. BH12—1D 22
Wharfedale Rd. BH4—4H 23
Wharncliffe Gdns. BH23—6B 18
Wharncliffe Rd. BH5—2G 27
Wharncliffe Rd. BH23—5B 18
Whatleigh Clo. BH15—6D 20
Wheaton Rd. BH7—1A 26
Wheeler's La. BH11—5C 4
Whitby Av. BH18—3B 8
Whitby Clo. BH23—1D 14
Whitby Cres. BH18—3B 8
Whitchurch Av. BH18—1E 9
Whitecliff Cres. BH14—5H 21
Whitecliff Rd. BH14—5G 21
White Clo. BH15—6A 10

Whitecross Clo. BH17—2F 9
White Farm Clo. BH10—5A 12
Whitefield Rd. BH14—5H 21
Whitefield Rd. BH25—2H 19
Whitehall. BH23—1H 27
Whitehayes Clo. BH23—3B 16
Whitehayes Rd. BH23—3A 16
White Horse Dri. BH15—2E 21
Whitehorses. BH25—6G 19
Whitehouse Rd. BH21—1F 3
White Knights. BH25—6H 19
Whiteleg Way. BH10—5B 6
Whitingham Rd. BH13—4E 23
Whitsbury Clo. BH8—3F 13
Whittles Way. BH15—5D 20
Wick Clo. BH25—3F 19
Wick Dri. BH25—3G 19
Wicket Rd. BH10—5H 5
Wickfield Clo. BH23—1H 27
Wickfield Clo. BH23—1H 27
Wick La. BH6—2G 27
Wick La. BH23—1H 27
Wicklea Rd. BH6—3H 27
Wickmeads Rd. BH6—2G 27
Widdicombe Av. BH14—5D 22
Wightworth Dri. BH18—5B 2
Wight Wlk. BH22—1A 6
Wilderton Rd. BH3—4E 23
Wilderton Rd. W. BH13—3F 23
Wildfell Clo. BH23—4G 15
Wildown Gdns. BH6—4G 27
Wildown Rd. BH6—4G 27
Wilfred Rd. BH5—2H 25
Wilkinson Dri. BH8—3B 14
Wilkins Way. BH15—5C 2
Willett Rd. BH21—1A 2 to 1E 3
William Clo. BH23—3C 18
William Rd. BH7—2H 25
Willis Way. BH15—1D 20
Willow Clo. BH4—2G 23
Willow Dri. BH23—2G 27
Willow Mead. BH9—6G 7
Willow Tree Rise. BH11—2G 11
Willow Way. BH23—2G 27
Wills Rd. BH12—2E 23
Willwood Clo. BH17—2F 9
Wilmur Cres. BH15—1G 21
Wilson Rd. BH1—1G 25
Wilson Rd. BH14—3B 22
Wilson Clo. BH23—4D 14
Wilton Gdns. BH25—2G 19
Wilverley Av. BH8—3H 13
Wilverley Rd. BH23—5E 17
Wimborne Minster By-Pass.
BH21—1D 2
Wimborne Rd. BH11, BH9,
BH3 & BH2—5E 5 to 3C 24
Wimborne Rd. BH15
—6D 8 to 4E 21
Wimborne Rd. BH3—6D 12
Windgreen Est. BH21—3A 2
Windham Rd. BH1—2E 25
Windsor Clo. BH5—3G 25
Windsor Rd. BH14—4A 22
Windsor Rd. BH25—5E 15
Winfrith Cres. BH12—5D 10
Wingfield Av. BH15—1F 21
Wingfield Av. BH23—3H 17
Winifred Rd. BH15—2F 21
Winkton Clo. BH23—2A 16
Winnards Clo. BH22—1B 6
Winsford Clo. BH23—3G 17
Winsley Av. BH6—3G 27
Winspit Clo. BH15—4A 20
Winston Av. BH12—6E 11
Winston Gdns. BH12—6F 11
Winston Rd. BH9—2D 12
Winterbourne Clo. BH15—2F 21
Winterbourne Rd. BH15—2F 21
Winterhayes Clo. BH17—2F 9
Wishart Gdns. BH9—6E 7
Wisteria Ho. BH10—1C 12
Witchampton Rd. BH18—3B 8
Withermoor Rd. BH9—5B 12

Woking Rd. BH14—2B 22
Wolfe Clo. BH23—6B 16
Wollaston Rd. BH6—4F 27
Wollstonecroft Rd. BH5—3H 25
Wolseley Rd. BH12—1C 22
Wolterton Rd. BH12—1F 23
Wolverton Rd. BH7—2H 25
Wonderholme Pde. BH11
—3G 11
Woodbury Av. BH8—3H 13
Woodbury Clo. BH23—2E 15
Woodcocks Cres. BH7—5B 14
Woodend Rd. BH9—5B 12
Woodfield Gdns. BH23—4H 17
Woodfield Rd. BH11—6F 5
Woodford Rd. BH1—3E 25
Woodgreen Dri. BH11—6C 4
Woodhayes Av. BH23—3H 17
Woodland Av. BH5—3A 26
Woodlands Av. BH15—4A 20
Woodlands Cres. BH15—4A 20
Woodlands Rd. BH25—6G 16
Woodland Wlk. BH5—3A 26
Woodland Way. BH23—5H 17
Wood La. BH11—5D 4
Wood Lawn Clo. BH25—5G 19
Woodleaze Clo. BH18—5D 2
Woodpecker Dri. BH17—5A 8
Woodside Rd. BH5—3B 26
Woodside Rd. BH14—4B 22
Woodstock Clo. BH15—5A 22
Woodstock Rd. BH14—5A 22
Woodstock Rd. BH23—2B 16
Woods View Rd. BH9—5A 12
Wool Rd. BH12—5A 10
Woolven Clo. BH14—2H 21
Wootton Mt. BH1—4D 24
Worbarrow Gdns. BH12—5B 10
Wordsworth Av. BH8—4G 13
Worgret Rd. BH15—6E 9
Worrell Dri. BH12—5B 10
Worthington Cres. BH14—4A 22
Worthy Rd. BH25—2H 19
Wortley Rd. BH23—5B 18
Wotton Gdns. BH1—4D 24
Wraxall Clo. BH17—4F 9
Wren Clo. BH23—2E 29
Wren Cres. BH12—2F 23
Wroxham Rd. BH12—2E 23
Wychwood Clo. BH2—3B 24
Wychwood Dri. BH2—2B 24
Wycliffe Rd. BH9—5C 12
Wykeham Clo. BH17—5G 9
Wyncombe Rd. BH5—2F 25
Wyndham Clo. BH23—3D 18
Wyndham Rd. BH14—4A 22
Wyndham Rd. BH23—3D 18
Wynford Rd. BH9—1D 12
Wynford Rd. BH14—3B 22
Wynne Clo. BH18—1B 8
Wynter Clo. BH7—5H 13
Wyvern Clo. BH12—5C 10

Yarmouth Clo. BH12—2F 23
Yarmouth Rd. BH12—1F 23
Yarrow Clo. BH23—5F 17
Yarrow Rd. BH17 & BH12
—5H 9 to 3A 10
Yeatminster Rd. BH17—3G 9
Yelverton Rd. BH1—4C 24
Yeomans Ind. Pk. BH8—3H 13
Yeomans Rd. BH8—3G 13
Yeomans Way. BH8—2G 13
York Clo. BH18—3C 8
York Clo. BH23—5F 15
York Pl. BH7—2H 26
York Rd. BH1—3E 25
York Rd. BH18—4B to 1C 8
Youngs Rd. BH11—6F 5

Zamek Clo. BH11—6F 5
Zinnia Clo. BH10—3A 12
Zinnia Gdns. BH10—3A 12